CLIFFORD HUMPHREY

PAGE PUBLISHING, INC.
New York, NY

First originally published by Page Publishing, Inc. 2019

ISBN 978-1-64544-284-4 (Paperback)
ISBN 978-1-64544-285-1 (Digital)

Printed in the United States of America

My name is Clifford Humphrey, and I came to prison a very sad and broken man, a slave to the devil's destructive drugs and alcohol. My addiction was out of control! I was on my way to death and hell at breakneck speed, and we all know that when we meet the grim reaper, death, and the very abyss of eternal hellfire, there is no return. Thanks and praises to the good Lord, he gave me a second chance at life by giving me a prison cell, because in prison, I still had life in my body and a chance to change my life for the better as it relates to societal change (where I respect the laws of man) and, most importantly, spiritual redemption (where I change for a better life here on earth and in the eternal world for peace with my God).

Many times we confuse our needs from our wants or desires, and when we do this, we often allow ourselves to fall prey to the ravages of drugs and alcohol abuse or addictions. Then we become victims of the horrific demons of substance and alcohol abuse, and when it escalates, it can become one epidemic of grave proportion. Like a pig greedily consumes slop, drugs and alcohol can and will consume everything we ever cherished before our sick addictions took over—such as, self-respect, respect for others, family, morality, material possessions, personal freedom, peace, sanity, and most importantly, our sobriety and spirituality. But there is hope for us when we learn to put our trust in our loving, merciful, graceful, forgiving, and Almighty God with complete abandon to self-pride. We will then start to see the good fruits of our faith in God start to change our once chaotic lives for the better. We will know solitude, bliss, confidence, success, sobriety, and a spiritual rebirthing and renewal such as we could ever dream or imagine all because we learned to trust God to direct our lives.

Now, because of the grace of God, we can walk a higher plane of existence where we see past our insecure and frail flesh and discover we have immortality within us. We now see everything with real eyes—spiritual eyes—where we can fully see God's true will and purpose for our otherwise carnal, blinded, and mundane lives. Now, through the power of God's spirit, we are able to do the supernatural, and every waking moment of every day has meaning now because we chose to trust in our God to deliver us from the devil's roller coaster of chaotic and destructive addiction.

When that roller coaster starts, pain, misery, and destruction sets in. We must say no to the lies of false security that the addiction to drugs and alcohol creates in our minds and realize that the false sense of security is a trick of the devil's design to destroy our lives by stealing our sobriety and, ultimately, our very own souls. Therefore, we must stop the madness and let God help us, rather than letting the devil trick us into self-medication where we make our addiction living problems with drugs and alcohol, rather than dealing with the reality of our sick living problem by admitting to ourselves and God that the problem is real and that we are at the mercy of the relentless demonic destruction of drugs and alcohol addiction.

We must give God free rein in our lives to find direction and the spiritual strength needed to truly walk the path of true daily spiritual sobriety in life. God is that great power we need to free us from the bondage of drug and alcohol slavery. God is a power who is outside of us and greater than us who can lead us to drug- and alcohol-free lives.

We must abandon all selfish pride and learn humility, selflessness, and reverence for God; only then will we learn to trust *him* who is our only hope from the devil's demons of horrific drugs and alcohol. When we start to trust God, we will start to reap the fruits of God's mercy and grace, which will restore us to sanity and provide us with peace, stability of life, total freedom of mind, body, and spiritual resurrection such as we have never experienced.

When God changes our spirits, we are no longer selfish people who believe that everything revolves around us; instead we recognize the needs of others—alas, it is not all about self, but others we now see as factor into the equation of life as well. We, through God's mercy and grace, have been given the spirit of selflessness; this is an inherent trait that God seeded in all his children. Now, with God's spirit, we can do battle with the prince of darkness who controls all the evil addictions of this world.

We have the mind and the spirit of Christ; we now realize that drug and alcohol addiction is childish as it relates to behavior and decision-making because it clouds one's thought process, thus making our choices those of selfishness and self-gratification at the cost of hurting self, family, friends, breaking the laws of the land, and most of all, breaking our spiritual bond and relationship with God himself.

I stress over and over again that we must remain faithful in our walk with God if we want to stay on the winning side against the devil and his demon's devices of drug and alcohol addiction. God alone is our only refuge, fortress, and safe house from the chaos and corruption by the devil's dope and liquor. God is a consummate winner; he can and will allow us to walk a progressive true daily sobriety path if we ask him for his help. God is the way to new life—psychologically, physically, and most of all, I continue to stress, a spiritual awakening such as we have never seen before in life. When we allow God to intervene in our lives, we will begin to realize just how much we have grown in the spirit because we lean not on our human fleshly understanding but on the supernatural spiritual power of Almighty God to work in our lives to break the bonds and clutches of drugs and alcohol we once had in our lives. We can relinquish forever our painful social crutches in life formerly known as drugs and alcohol, but we can only conquer our addictions by trusting God and stepping out in faith to face our addictions head-on without fear and with complete honesty to ourselves, others, and most of all, God.

We must release ourselves from every fear, all guilt and shame, and with complete abandon free our addiction realistically and honestly. If we are not able to accept God's help against drug and alcohol addiction, we will suffer the pangs of hell on earth because when an addiction has run its course, it will eat, chew, and swallow up everything we ever valued most in life. Then, and only then, most of us will begin to realize the severity of our sick addiction. It takes for many of us to reach the brink, or utter collapse, or rock-bottom, before we can see the magnitude of our problem with addiction. Rock bottom, if you would, differs from person to person. As for me, my rock-bottom was coming to a prison cell all because of my wrong choices and my out-of-control behaviors, which were primary results or by-products of the drugs and alcohol I chose to consume.

Because of my horrific addiction to drugs and alcohol, I went to prison for the first time in my adult life. While in prison, I learned to look not to my own understanding but to that of a supernatural divine nature. Yes, I learned to depend on Almighty God himself, and with total surrender to God, I learned to also respect other people in life and to respect and learn discipline from my authority figures. God has never let me down. He has supplied my every need. When I was empty and even in despair, God filled me with his spirit. God set me free—mind, body, and soul, and he can do the same thing for every one of us if we ask and then remain spiritually strong.

Through God's amazing mercy and grace, we can defeat the addiction of Satan and know sobriety and peace on a continual basis. We must stay faithful to God so that he helps us to pave our road from addiction back to a real life of sanity and sobriety. God and God alone has the healing power to save and free our lives from the devil's addictions; therefore, we must call out to him for his help now, for tomorrow may be too late. We must ask God the Father to chastise us and bring us back into his fold as his legitimate children. If we belong to God, he will chastise his children to bring us back into his perfect will. God chastised me by giving me a prison cell to open the eyes of my deepest spiritual understanding. I began to see past my flesh. I started to see with real eyes—yes, spiritual eyes. I began to see the exact nature of my wrong, and I began to see the truth of God and his mercy and grace for me and the profound lies of Satan and the wicked drugs he used to destroy my life to the point of prison. Now I know I need God to live sober, stable, and sane, for this is the will of God. I'm ready to reintegrate into the mainstream of society fully focused on doing whatever is necessary to maintain my own freedom. I want to also go back to society and reflect the knowledge that I've absorbed while incarcerated. I want to shine forth as a bright light, as a true beacon of hope, and inspiration to all addicts who suffer and are still suffering. I want them to find the sobriety and peace that I've found through God, and with the help of others, I was influenced to do what was ultimately necessary, which was to change. I'm leaving past mistakes behind, and I'm building on renewed thoughts today, thoughts of positivity. People, if you want a new life of sobriety and peace, you must be willing to change.

Change is our only option. I'm so glad to be reconnected to my God: sobriety and sanity. Change has made it all possible. All things are possible with God and change. God has taught me that all my excuses and resentments in life were falsehoods used as self-manufactured defense mechanisms designed to help me protect, justify, and rationalize my sick drug and alcohol addiction. Having been exposed to drugs and alcohol on a daily basis in the penal system, I count it all joy that I've not had the slightest urge to relapse, but I realize that my true test will come upon my release into the free world, where I'll be tested by fixe, so to speak. But I have faith in God and faith in myself. Because I have within my heart a new spirit, a changed spirit, and with change and God, all things are possible. With change we can know sobriety, peace, and anything else we set our minds to achieve. If we want change, God can and will help us. God will provide a safe haven and refuge from the fiery pits of hell, if we abandon the devil's addictive drugs and alcohol and call out to God and change. We can escape death, the grave, and hell, for there are so many that didn't. Fact of the matter is that death, the grave, and hell are their reality right now, and the others who were lucky made it to prison. At least from a prison, we'll have life and a second chance to live life more abundantly.

I'm one of the many others lucky enough to live to see prison for a second chance at life and not to wind up an unfortunate victim of the grim reaper from whence there is no return. I'm amongst men most blessed. I have the breath of life and a godly renewed spirit. I respect the sunrise and all the beautiful majestic creations of God. It's time to put our common sense and faith to work and start to think before we act. I coined the phrase "think before acting" from my A+D substance abuse counselor, Mr. Jeff Nance. It makes good sense too! Jeff said that if we think before we act, 50 percent of our problems would never transpire or surface.

At the same time, we must also consider that sometimes life isn't fair and things happen beyond our control. We must remain vigilant and adaptable to whatever happens and take the bitter with the sweet. I know this to be fact, especially when a problem arises where we break the laws of the land, or sobriety, because of our addiction to drugs and alcohol. We must learn to accept responsibility for our problems and not point our fingers at the system, blaming them and not ourselves for the crimes we committed to bring us to prison.

It was our own bad choices and not the system that brought us to prison. The system didn't send for us; we came to prison for the crimes we committed of our own accord. On the flip side of the coin, even though the system didn't send for us, they should still be required to treat us like human beings and not just numbers. We're not wards of the state who are void of all human emotions and feelings that connect us to civil society. We, too, like the rest of the world, are people with human emotions. The only difference between us and the rest of society is that we broke the law and got caught, but we are paying our debt to society with a prison sentence and giving up our citizenship and other liberties that would be afforded to us if we were in the free world.

Therefore this should be punishment enough. We as human beings should never be stripped of our human dignity and treated like barbaric, uncivilized beasts void of intellect and beyond the possibility of ever being rehabilitated and reconnected to society as rational, civil, honest, self-reliant, law-abiding, and God-fearing people.

All these things are within our grasp if we are willing to change. So as people and not just as prisoners, we are faced with the choices of right and wrong. Good choices need to be made in our lives now because it was bad choices that turned us to addiction, crime, prison, and for some, death.

As I reflect on my past wrong or bad choices, I can clearly see what I need to do now to maintain my own freedom, and change is the only surefire option or solution. I am starting the process of change right here right now, from prison, by utilizing my time to gain knowledge and people skills to help me grow increasingly stronger, to ensure that I will be a success in prison, as well as out of prison. You see, we must start the change from the inside to the outside. If we can do this, we will be able to walk in our sobriety daily a spiritual path of lifelong sobriety with confidence and faith in God with complete success. By changing our thoughts, we change our lives. If we change our thoughts from bad to good, we will find that we can maintain our own freedom.

God will guide our every step because God is a God of right and good choices. God will punish those who choose to make wrong and bad choices. Always remember that we must surround ourselves with nonaddictive people who are positive about sobriety and success in life. Positivity breeds positivity, and a positive change brings unlimited potential for success in our lives, whereas no change leaves us in a constant state of negativity where we fail to evolve from our addiction and we bury ourselves in lifelong failures because we refuse to change from our old destructive thoughts.

Change is the only solution; with it we begin to think positively and realistically. When we are realistic thinkers, we will start to identify and recognize the triggers of our addictions; thus we will be able to successfully control our addictions. We must always remember that we, as addicts, are always only a drink and a drug away from relapse; therefore; we should celebrate each day of our sobriety with grace in the knowledge that God has given us another day.

If we continue to trust God, he will give us the spiritual strength and intestinal fortitude needed to be victorious over addiction where we can lead a life of progressive daily spiritual and lifelong sobriety. With God at our beckoning call, we can war daily against the demonic forces of drugs and alcohol and win the battle. Alas, we must always be aware of our surroundings as it relates to the wrong type of friends.

Addictive friends will only temp us down our old addictive lifestyle of chaos and corruption, and the wrong surrounding or environment is likely to trigger addictive behavior in us because of the fact that that type of environment will be one of which the criminal elements exist, ready and willing to sell us the product of our addictions. These things are all negative and dangerous to us as addicts; therefore, we must avoid them at all costs because our freedom and sobriety are worth far more than our addictions.

We need to make amends that are sober in order to reinforce our sobriety change. We can find these amends of sobriety in good, wholesome churches and neighborhoods that promote drug- and alcohol-free communities and drug and alcohol therapeutic counseling programs. All these things are good choices for us because they offer a support system to help aid us in our daily recovery; after all, our progress in sobriety is daily and even a lifelong progress, but we can stay the course if we are willing to take advantage of change. Change, like anything in life, requires effort, sacrifice, and most of all, obedience where we can embrace a sober lifestyle one of peace, sanity, and success; therefore, we must be willing to be receptive to change and allow ourselves to be helped by God and all the people he will use to benefit us in life.

When we accept change as our only option and give God free rein, he will give us complete freedom from our otherwise-confusing lives. God has all power, and he can and will deliver us from all addictions. He is ready to save us whenever we call. God will never forsake us, though our lives may endure many stripes and tribulations. Just know, it's all part of God's perfect plan to bring us back into his perfect will.

God will give us good things in life if we endure the storms of life. We must accept chastisement with grace because God corrects all his children only to make them complete and whole again. Yes, even in our darkest hour of despair, God will always be there for us ready to deliver us and bring us back from addiction's abyss where we can reap the fruits of his favor with a life of sobriety, stability, sanity, and spirituality. You see, all these things are within our reach if we are willing to change.

God allows storms, trials, and tribulations to test us in life in order to increase and fortify our trust and faith in him. When we walk by faith, we can do the impossible in life; therefore, we must believe that our faith in our change can renew us and give us real eyes of the spirit, strong enough to see past our weak mortal flesh. When we peer through the eyes of profound spirituality, we see beyond the external. We begin to see things in a whole new light. We see with the eyes of the eternal man, who is the immortal man. The immortal man, or the spirit man, is able to believe through faith the awesome miracles God is ready to perform.

If we rise above our fleshly disbelief, we can witness the supernatural miracles of an all-powerful God, who's willing to help us change our lives for the better. Although change is necessary, God never promised that it would a bed of roses, but with God in our lives, the good will surely outweigh the bad in our lives. When we allow God to work in our lives, he will change our every circumstance for good. God will, in fact, put people in our lives to aid us; they will be people who are spiritual, sober, humble, sane, honest, financially successful, and of good moral character. These people can help us to reshape and remold the course of our lives as it relates to maintaining our sobriety, freedom, sanity, and becoming a success in whatever career goals we decide to pursue, and most of all, they can help us to become well-rounded individuals and complete spiritual beings.

God will, indeed, bless all his children with all the things we need in life and more. All we have to do is have faith and total trust in him, and by this simple act of obedience, God will shower us with his many blessings and allow us to prosper at whatever we touch. God will surround us with the elites of society no matter where we are: prison, free world, or wherever his blessings will continue. He rewards those who obey him and diligently seek him. As long as we walk in the light of truth, we can know sobriety and peace and God's hand will always protect us.

God will work through people and angels to help us, and he will provide every situation to help us; it may be a church, a rehabilitation center, a book of twelve-step programs, help from other addicts who suffer from the same addictions as ourselves, or even the visitation from an angel who may come to you with a message unawares—all this if we remain faithful and obedient to God. He will bless us and never let us down. God is truly an awesome God, and I will be ever thankful to him for his unconditional love and mercy, without which

I would not be able to change my life as I continue on my daily road of sobriety.

When we give God our all—yes, total complete surrender—we will know a life of bliss where we have sobriety, peace, sanity, and the very spirit of God. Only God can free us from the slave chains of drugs and alcohol. You see, every one of us has within us a sleeping giant, and when he is awakened, he is capable of great things in life. People, that sleeping giant is the spiritual us, the real us, and when we are awakened, we can change our lives for the better.

We can succeed in our every endeavor if we wake up to the reality of who we really are in God. God wants us all to come to the knowledge of the truth. When we do this, then we can reap God's favor and grace. We will be able to live our lives in sobriety, sanity, and peace. We will have total joy through the redemptive healing power of God when we finally see with spiritual eyes that the flesh alone can do nothing but it is the spirit that enables us to do all things because with God all things are possible, including defeating the deep, dark hellish addictions called drugs and alcohol. Only through our faith and trust in God and complete selfless, humble submission and obedience can we expect God to exalt us to the high level of sobriety and peace; therefore, if we want this great gift from God, we must forever abandon pride and selfishness and give up fleeting pleasures that lead to death and destruction.

Yes, we must give up that monster of destruction called drugs and alcohol; if we don't, we will suffer the eternal wrath of God and be forever debased or brought low to the fiery abyss of hell. As a rational and logical human being, who, being enlightened spiritually, would much rather God exalt them for the good than to be finally cut down by God and go to hell for eternity for disobedience; therefore, we must flee from the devil and his deceptive, wicked drugs and alcohol that lead to deadly addiction. Today I choose my sobriety and peace that God so mercifully bestowed upon me. God is the door whereby we enter into the kingdom of eternal peaceful bliss.

God will only allow entry to those of us who truly want salvation. Within that door we can find absolute freedom and blissful peace. We can finally be free from the prison of hatred, resentment, being unforgiving, and most of all, we can be free from the prison of disbelief in the redemptive power of an Almighty God; therefore, with unshakeable faith, we press on toward our spiritually guided sobriety, with thanks and prayers to our almighty and never-failing God.

If we expect to ever live normal lives, free from the clutches of the devil's addictive drugs and alcohol, we must become selfless, humble, and obedient servants to God and man—that is, when God will hear from heaven and he will take control of our lives and give us the will to strive daily and progressively toward our sobriety. Only God can give us grace to find the spiritual intestinal fortitude that can usher us on to sobriety, sanity, peace, and spiritual completeness. We must never lean on our own human frailty with expectations of finding solutions to our addiction. Man is far too weak and limited because of his mortality; therefore, it is impossible for us as mortal men to fight and win the battle of addiction on our own.

So we must call on the power of Almighty God who is able to do all things for he is God. God is the key to everything in life on earth and the life to come eternal. You see, God is a power far greater than ourselves and outside of ourselves, who is able to deliver us from any and all addictions in life. God has blessed us with the ability to rise above the limitation of the flesh because God gave us all a spirit that is eternal in nature. With this immortal spirit, we know that we are not the sum of our biology, because the spirit is above the flesh. With the spirit, we can change our lives for the better and prove to all humanity that our lives aren't shaped by our genes or biology. I'm glad that our Father God gave us a spirit of immortality, enabling us to do great things in life. God made us conquerors; therefore, we should never be slaves to anything or anyone in life. Drugs and alcohol are no exception to the rule. God the Father is always strong and never weak. When we cast our complete faith in him, we can tap into his strength and find his redemptive grace and abounding eternal grace.

God is all we need to help us pursue a progressive daily spiritual path of sobriety full of hope and promise in life. When we begin to tap into the power of God's abundant grace, we can continue in the knowledge that we are rooted and grounded with the right ingredient, which is God's Word, that will give us the strength to stay our course of sobriety. It's all up to the choices we make in life. We can choose the chaotic destruction of drugs and alcohol that leads to prison, death, and hell, or we can choose sobriety and peace away from drugs and alcohol that will give us lasting sobriety and peace in this life and life eternal.

As for me, I choose the good life of sobriety and peace. God is my pilot in all I do in life; therefore, he will make sure that I'm not destroyed by drugs and alcohol abuse. We can know the ecstatic joy of sobriety and the unspeakable peace of sobriety where we submit to the authority of our higher power God. God is an ever-present rock and refuge from the insanity of addiction. Every day of sobriety is a victory, so we must give thanks to God because it was by his will and good grace that we were able to see that day. As long as we focus on God and not on our own weak flesh, we will remain constant and will know that we are on the right track as it relates to our continual sobriety.

We can realize our dreams through sobriety. When we are sober, our eyes—that is, our true spiritual eyes—are clear; the fog is gone, and we see perfectly clear. All our dreams are now within our reach. We are refreshed and renewed through God's mercy and grace. Whether we are physically fine or not, we should still plan for a future of sobriety where we are drug-free, prison-free, chaos-free, and most of all, spiritually free. In finding freedom like this, we make peace with ourselves, our fellow man, and God. Where we can once again gain the respect and love of family and friends, then all will be right with us and God and the world about us.

As I write this book, I sit in prison, but I know that I'll soon be free because my God is Almighty and he has all authority; therefore, my God has the final word, and he can bring me out whenever he choose. Man only has the power to imprison our bodies, but he can never imprison the mind. We are in control of our own minds, so our thoughts can never be held captive, for they are immortal. There is no prison of man worthy to hold them captive because they are of God; therefore, we must realize our God gives authority through the spirit to plot our own destinies in life. If we make godly choices, we will find sobriety and peace free from the turmoil and devastation that addiction can cause in our lives.

When we abandon the slave chains of addiction, we will know true freedom of mind, body, and soul, basking in the glory of daily and progressive sobriety. Yes, we can know this life if we allow God to nourish our spirit. Only by God's favor, mercy, and grace can we obtain this gift. God is knocking at the very door of our hearts; all we have to do is let him in. We all know that this is what we need, but we must be willing to make that choice to change for the better, because only a fool would choose to live a life of hell on earth addicted to the devil's destructive drugs and alcohol and then die and go to an eternal spiritual hell where we will be tormented forever by the devil's hellfire that can never be quenched.

The choice is ours. As for me, I choose to change for the better in my present life, where I can reap God's favor, grace, and mercy in this life and the next. You see, I want to experience the bliss of peace, sobriety, and sanity here and now where I can be free to live a life outside of prison with my family where I can enjoy my dignity, material possessions, and freedom from a self-imposed psychological prison, and lastly, I want to be able to know that I will have eternal rest in the life to come by making sure that God is in charge of every facet of my life—meaning that my spirituality is well-balanced.

I'm going to stay the course of daily, progressive spiritual sobriety, making sure that my body, mind, and soul are in God's hands where I can be assured a life of abundance for the here and now and the life to come eternal.

God can and will help us if we allow him. My life is a living testimony of what God can do to renew one's life for the better. I am going to use my life's experiences, trials, and tribulations—written down on paper and with ink, in the form of street poetic prose—in a sincere effort to promote thoughts for positive change and healing choices to bring lasting peace, sobriety, and sanity to the lives of other people at the mercy of addiction, chaos, insanity, and unmanageable lives.

The Streets

I used to push a lac and even sold crack
My lac floated on trues and vogues
I ran with nothing but thugs and rogues
My lac had a crunk sound that banged from the trunk
That made ya wanna do yo own dance and junk
When ya mention that cheddar cheese that hard, cold cash
I had the mumps in my pocket I had more than a playa's stash
When I would dress, man, was I the dapper don
Dressed to impress
And heaven knows I played the ladies I used to call hoes
I lived for the bling blang
My neck was draped with a treasure chest of gold chains
And on every finger including my pinky
I played the bling of diamond and gold rangs and thangs
Every day of my life was always bling bling
Pagers blowing up and my cell phone was constantly ring ring
Living large in a world of crime, it never crossed my mind that I
    could be doing time
Cause when we are having fun, we tend to believe we are living life
    and fear none
But one day I realized my sin and fell down on my knees
And asked God to forgive me please
Now I don't seek the material, you see
Now I know it is God I need to be rich and free

The Wrong Way

As a little boy I was a man
I was always rough and like to take my stand
I came up in a world of crime and found myself caught up in my prime
As I grew older, I became bolder then went from flipping twenty
    rocks in the hood
To slanging weight and driving lacs with trues and vogue
And banging sound and nailing any chicken head I could
I walked around, drove around, parlayed around, always ready to snap
I carried a strap with one always chambered
I was on point to bust cop
My set was thugs, rogues, and hoes
For the world of money, I made many foes
But after turning to the very dope I sold
I lost everything I owned
Including my self-respect and respect for others
I really grew cold
Nowhere to turn but to other crime
But the next road of wrong led me to a prison cell where I'm doing
    time
No longer do I choose the wrong way
God has shown me the light and never again will I go astray
I was lucky not to wind up in a grave, you see
At least from a prison cell, I can be rehabilitated and free

Po man in the ghetto wanna get out
Po man in the ghetto wanna get out
Po man in the ghetto searching every route
Always bad news
Enough to give you the blues
In the slum tenements I see the rats and roaches crawling
Then hear the babies for milk squealing
Po man in the ghetto went look for a job
But everywhere he went was but many a snob
Po man in the ghetto at the end of his rope perchance to sell dope
Then he thought about prison
So this wasn't a good decision
Alas, he fell down and prayed to God on his knees
And said, "God, help me please"
God gave ear to him and said, "I give you now the keys
Which are all of these
Stay strong in spirit, humility, faith, and love
And I will give you all things from above"
Po man in the ghetto found his way
He is educating himself to this very day

Cocaine

When I first took a hit of crack
For me it was no going back
The crack knew my name
And called me to ruin and shame
Crack consumed everything of value that I ever had
Leaving me broke and sad
Cocaine brought me a world of pain
I was just about to go insane
The call of crack became so strong
It led me to cheat, steal, rob, and do all manner of wrong
Then God made a way for all this madness to stop
One gracious day, he sent an angel dressed like a cop
And on another day, God sent an angel dressed like a judge
He rescued me, and for that I am thankful and without a grudge
For he saved my life by giving me a prison cell
Because I was out of control and on my way to hell
God and his angels of mercy saved me
Now I respect God and my fellow man, and I am ready to be free
I will honor the laws of God and men
And never come to prison again

THANKS FOR READING THE POETIC trials and tribulations of my life. Now I hope that in reading my story, you come away with a message of hope for a positive change for your lives where peace, sobriety, and sanity will prevail. You see, we all make bad choices and mistakes at one point in all our lives, but we mustn't dwell on them but rather reflect on them so we can break the cycle and start making good, healthy choices in our lives that will help us be responsible and productive citizens with the heart and desire to break the slave chains of addiction.

Therefore, we must make the choice to get up when we fall if we care ever to free ourselves from the prison of addiction. We must learn to trust in God as our source for strength. With God's help we can stand and battle and even defeat the devil's addiction. I've seen hellfire in the streets, and against all odds, I made it through all the trials and tribulations in those mean and wicked streets. I sold dope, used dope, drank plenty of alcohol—man, I've literally seen it all.

Even as I write this manual I struggle, yet I praise and I thank God because life is precious, and it's a good day to be alive even if I'm in prison because I have life and a second chance at freedom outside of prison as opposed to some—like two of my best friends a.k.a. Skee-bop and G-man. They are in the federal pin with drug kingpin convictions. They will never touch free-world soil with their feet ever again because they have life sentences. What a tragic turn or twist of fate. One moment they are kingpins in the drug world living large in the lap of pleasure and illicit luxury. Then the next moment they spiral down and see all their ill-gotten material acquisitions take flight like birds in flight; everything quickly soars away and disappears out of sight. Like evil street kings they have fallen from their self-appointed thrones, only to be thrown into a federal prison cell where they will never rise by way of corruption ever again. Fact of the matter is, life as they once knew it is over, all because of a bad choice and their inability to learn from prison mistakes or bad choices. They were not willing to change for the better.

Actions always have consequences; therefore, we all should learn to think before we act in order that we may avert potentially life-ruining consequences. If we all can learn to think about our choices prior to acting rashly on them then, perhaps we won't make a choice in life that ultimately destroys our lives, like my two best friends, Skee-Bop and G-man, did.

I thank my higher power God for giving me the right situation that brought about a severing of my drug-dealing ties with my two friends all in due time. Because if not for that divine intervention, I would be facing life in the federal pin with my friends instead of the state sentence I have where I will soon be free, unlike Skee-Bop and G-man who are facing life and life with the feds. People, having said all this, I believe that common sense should urge us all to want to change for the better and think before we act so we can make good choices in life where we won't wind up imprisoned for life or become lifelong addicts enslaved to drugs and alcohol that will eventually steal our peace and cause chaos, insanity, and eventually death. As for me, I've had enough heartache and negativity in my life caused by making bad choices that led me to consume drugs and alcohol where I finally became addicted to them to the point of where I lost respect for myself and others. It, in turn, caused me to become selfish, and all I wanted to do is do whatever it took to get the next high, whether it meant committing a crime or not; at the time it really didn't seem to matter.

That's why I'm doing prison time right now, and I wish now that I'd thought prior to making that bad choice because I know now that everything matters and that every action has a consequence that not only affects us but also the lives of others as well. Therefore, we must make wise choices in our lives starting with turning to God.

May we all learn to surrender to God and let him order every step we take in our lives.

Let us repent of our sins and learn from our bad choices in life. When we trust in God, our prayers will never be ignored. He will heal our minds, spirits, and our bodies. We will be completely restored. God can do anything because he is supernatural, divine, immortal, self-created, self-existent, and almighty. God is more than I can describe in words; he mustn't be put in a box because he has no bounds or limits.

Only mortal weak man is limited because he is flesh and born to die and see corruption. Our unlimited Lord never saw corruption. God the Son is on the right hand of God the Father interceding for us right now, and if we trust and depend on him, he will see us through all our trials and lead us to everlasting happiness if we let him. It's our choice, so let's choose wisely and cast our faith in God and follow his Word of truth, the Holy Bible. This source of truth eternal, supernatural and supreme, turned my life around.

I went from drug seller, user, and robber to a born-again Christian soldier, and if he can do this for me, he can do it for any-body who asks and believes that he can through faith. Therefore, if we are to find peace, sobriety, and sanity that will last, we must abandon the notion that we can do it alone because man is sure to fail, but God can never fail. All we need is to trust him, so in the spirit of faith, let us look to God as our refuge and guide toward a successful life full of hope, peace, sobriety, and sanity.

When we, as addicts, start to step out in faith and depend on God, we can be sure that God will reward us with a multitude of blessings to where we will even exceed our every expectation in life. We can rejoice together in a state of blissful normalcy, where we have hope, peace, sanity, and we are content with our blessed sobriety with our newfound spirit of productivity, drug- and alcohol-free. Therefore, let us press on toward all these things in the hopes to lay hold on these true treasures and know a lasting peace through our higher power, God. But we mustn't forget that we can only have these things by letting God pilot our lives.

Always remember that we must always be willing to admit that we have an addiction problem to ourselves and others, then admit to

God that we have no control; therefore, we humbly ask that he save our lives from our chaotic and destructive addictions.

God the Father is always strong and never weak, and if we cast our faith in him, we can experience his healing grace and his spiritual strength that will guide us successfully through every obstacle in life, including the wicked deceptive tools of the devil called drugs and alcohol. We know God is our only hope to maintain our sobriety, but God will always leave the choice up to us. As for me, I choose my higher power, who's an all-powerful God, who is able to bring all our hopes for love, peace, freedom, spirituality, and prosperity to fruition in our lives.

Every day we complete sober is a day in which we should rejoice because this lets us know we are on the right track in life, and through God's good grace, we can realize attainable goals in our lives. Whether we are physically free or in bonds, we should plan for a future of sobriety where we are drug- and alcohol-free, prison-free, chaos-free, and at peace with ourselves where our friends and family respect and love us again and all is right with us and God and the world about us. God has the final word in every life, so even if we are in prison, God can bring us out when he chooses to do so.

Society can never imprison our minds or our spiritual essence; therefore, we, through the grace of God, plot the course of our own destinies; and if we make godly choices in our lives, we will find that we can live our lives free of drugs and alcohol and the turmoil and the destruction that come with them. Drug and alcohol abuse is never worth all the hellish problems that come with it—especially when they send us to prison away from our family; strip us of our dignity, spirituality, material possessions; and cause us to live in a self-imposed psychological and spiritual prison.

Our only escape is for us to get a grip and turn to God for help to keep from losing our very souls. God delivers all wayward repented souls. He can and will deliver us even in our darkest and seemingly most hopeless hour if we choose to humbly ask. We all need to step outside of our humanistic arrogance and selfish pride and give our higher power, God, his just, deserving reverence and exaltation. For we must remember, God is the supreme creator of the universe, and all things were spoken into existence by his Word. God the Son, the Father, and the Holy Spirit are but one God—our God—from whence we all came forth, when he spoke his Word. Now, with all this knowledge, we should be quick to follow God's Word that was written by his inspired prophets as a tool, or rather, what I would like to call, God's "owner's manual to life." If we read this owner's manual, which is God's Holy Bible, we will find peace, sobriety, and sanity, even a completeness that mere words cannot describe.

The Word is nourishing food for our souls, and we should eat of God's Word daily so that we may live life more abundantly and taste salvation with God for all eternity. If we follow God's owner's manual in our lives, we can reach maximum enlightenment, therefore enabling us to conquer the frail temptations of the flesh. With the spirit, man at the helm, we can be victorious in our every trial in life. Drugs and alcohol will be no exception, so let us build a fortress around ourselves with God's Word of refuge and salvation.

God's owner's manual, the Holy Bible, can lead us in the path of righteousness and not in the chaotic path of drugs and alcohol. So I say, let God be true, and every frail, weak, fleshly willed man be a liar, for God is the author of all that is decent and righteous. He isn't a God of confusion and chaos; therefore, we, through the gift of his righteous spirit, should continue to conquer the flesh and pursue our sobriety on a daily yet progressive basis.

When we allow ourselves to submit to the will of God, we lay hold on God's spiritual strength that enables us to battle the demons of drugs and alcohol abuse by walking in spiritual sobriety under the Bible, which is God's owner's manual for our lives. We can aspire to every level of prosperity that God intended for us in life. The manual will add new direction, hope, salvation, freedom from all addictions, solidarity of all love relationships, and every other good thing your mind could ever imagine possible.

I would rather live a life of godliness and happiness than to live a life of hell and then die and go to a devil's hell. God is truth, life, and light. The devil is lie, death, and darkness. The devil is full of lies, deception, and hate. His primary purpose is to steal, kill, and destroy. I know for a fact that drugs and alcohol do all the aforementioned; therefore, they are of the devil. We must choose God and walk in truth, righteousness, and light, where we can be sober and clean. Looking through real eyes, eyes of sobriety and sanity, always remember: God's children will do his will. That will is to live a life of sobriety, faith, focus, and purpose, as opposed to one of chaos, destruction, confusion, and drug and alcohol addiction.

When we, as spiritual sobriety seekers and believers of God, can unite together for the common good and goal of sobriety and the worship of God, we can fight the demons of drug and alcohol abuse. God is fighting for every sober and faithful soul, but the devil is fighting to make every drug and alcohol addict's life bitter and cold. We, as logical human beings, must free ourselves of every addiction in life, in order that we be free mentally, physically, and most of all, spiritually. God is a spirit, and he requires that we worship him in spirit and in truth. As for me, I surely will because God was merciful enough toward me to give me another chance at a more abundant life. He redeemed me from an earthly hell, saved me from an early grave, and most of all, he saved me from eternal damnation, which is everlasting spiritual hell.

I've now relinquished all my addictions. I'm serving my Lord and Savior Jesus Christ sober and with a humble spirit. God wants us all to know peace, sobriety, and happiness. He said in Jeremiah 29:11, "I know the thoughts that I think toward you, saith the Lord," thoughts of peace and not evil, to give you an expected, and therefore, it's high time we abandon the use of demonic drugs and alcohol in our lives because they steal all our hopes and dreams for a good life. If we adhere to God's owner's manual in life, we will know new vision. With that vision, we can find our way down the path of a life that is drug- and alcohol-free.

A life full with God's blessings of peace, love, spirituality, freedom from all prisons of mind, body, and soul, we can know eternal bliss if we are willing to submit to God who is our higher power. To continue the path of drugs and alcohol would be like playing Russian roulette with one's life. Whenever we spin the pistol chamber and prior to pulling that trigger of surprise, we don't know if we'll catch that fatal bullet, causing us instant death. I choose not to play that cruel game with my life because life is precious. Because God created it, therefore we must forge ahead and meet all our addictions head-on without a mask. We must be brutally honest with ourselves as it relates to our addictions because then, and only then, will we search and find the spiritual power deep within our inner man, given to us by God himself to fight every evil thing that would oppose his children.

So I'm convinced that the evils of drugs and alcohol can be defeated if we fight the battle through God. Remember, too, if we keep on drugging and drinking, that revolving door to prison will continue to revolve bringing us back and forth to lonely prison cells. There will be some, though, who will not make it back to prison; the ultimate fate may overtake them, and that fate my friend is the "Grim Reaper," who will send us to our graves because he is "Mr. Death."

There is no return from the watery grave. There are no more chances for redemption there. Drug and alcohol use, if we continue, will cause death and destruction every time. We must be real about the nature of our addictions and at the same time be responsible for our addictions. When we discover the exact nature of our addictions and shoulder the responsibility for our own addictions, we can start to grow in maturity and evolve to a level of sanity, peace, sobriety, spirituality, and security in our lives. We will have then learned to accept our addictions without blaming others for them.

Through the grace of a loving God, we can walk the path of true spiritual sobriety on a daily and progressive basis. Through our higher power, God, we have the power to tap into that spiritual inner man within us to battle the daily temptations of drugs and alcohol. Beating our addictions won't be a walk in the park, but all things are possible with God.

God said his grace is sufficient for thee, and his strength is made perfect in our weakness, so when we admit that we are frail and weak and can do nothing without him, that's when his grace will make us strong, even in our weakness. Because this grace is the strength that will make our weak, frail bodies stand strong. Always remember this: man's wisdom is foolishness to God; therefore, we must conclude man's intellect is far less than the unlimited intellect of the higher power, God.

When we accept God in our lives, we can free ourselves of any and all denials in life; whether addiction or whatever, we can be free where we can safely explore new avenues and ideas in life that will allow overall growth in a positive direction. We must strive to grow into mature adults by staying sober because a lifetime of addiction causes one to never reach maturity, be it psychologically, spiritually, or emotionally. Failure to stop our addiction to drugs and alcohol can prevent us from ever becoming mature emotional beings. What we need is to be possessed by the truth about ourselves and our higher power, God, in order that we reach, or rather maintain, our daily and even lifelong sobriety. With our own humanistic truths, there is no way we can ever harness real spiritual, godly truth, freely given by God to those of us who are his and are spiritual and daily seek his grace.

God's truth is the spiritual real truth that leads to pure salvation and freedom from any and all addictions. Humanistic truths are fleshly falsehoods that lead us toward imprisonment of mind, body, and soul. We must remain vigilant in our quest for our sobriety by choosing God and the spiritual truth he has given to his believers. Humanistic truths forever fall short of what we need for true sobriety, vision, and purpose in life.

So I'm choosing the high road through God because I seek to become a better person than I was when I went to prison. Through God's guidance, we should all want to do this because most of us are confused, negative, and displaced people, and we are known by others as such, because of our addiction to drugs and alcohol. It's time to break the cycle and start to do positive things in life and rely on the help of our higher power to guide us and deliver us from every evil in life, even the evils of drug and alcohol addiction.

Alcohol and drug addiction is a big lie. They induce false pride, false security, and utter chaos. We all know these are things we don't need in our lives. We would be foolish to succumb to mind-altering drugs and alcohol because all the aforementioned things are nothing but deceptive tricks to consume our lives by the "devil" himself.

Sobriety and humility are the keys to the good life where we can realize spiritual, mental, and physical freedom in our lives.

God favors and exalts the humble, and he resists and abases the proud; therefore, I will walk in spirituality and humility and await God's blessings and not walk with fleshly pride and experience God's wrath. Whenever we feel weak in our walk of sobriety, all we need to do is call on our higher power, God, for help, and he will give us the spiritual strength we need to persevere and be responsible individuals who are ready and willing to wake up from a once-deep sleep, ready to conquer the plagues of addiction by becoming a real family man. We need to maintain our freedom of mind, body, and soul, respecting the laws of the land, maintaining our sobriety, and most of all, we must maintain a personal relationship with God.

I have experienced drinking and drugging. I never got the same high the second time as I did the first time, so why would I, using common sense, keep chasing cocaine vapor demons over and over again, hoping to experience that first high? That first high will never ever happen a second time.

Drug and alcohol addiction have devastated the lives of untold millions with broken homes, lost lives, addictive lives, and overcrowded prisons. This is insanity, and we need to stop the madness now. Tomorrow may be too late. The addictions of drugs and alcohol are menacing and destructive to the lives of all they touch. Addictions alter the mindset to the point where we feel no compassion for self or human life. We commit criminal acts as if they were second nature, whereas if we were in our sober state of mind, where God is in control, then we wouldn't have committed those horrible crimes without natural compassion for self and others.

We have the capacity to change our addictive lifestyles if we admit to ourselves and others that we have a problem and then ask God to help us with our problem. We must be willing to step out in faith to help ourselves, and then God will help us. He will hear us then he will start to heal us. God helps those who help themselves. We should remember that we all have a story that we must tell to someone, someday.

Today, as I write this manual, I'm telling mine. I hope with all my being that all who read my manual will come away with something they can use to make their lives better as it relates to the continuity of peace, sobriety, and sanity. When we have all those things we can have healthy relationships with our families, ourselves, society, and most importantly, God.

We can then begin to heal by forgiving ourselves and others for past wrongs, hurts, and resentments, and when we start to do these things God will, in turn, forgive us. We must learn not to blame others for our bad choices in life and say that he, she, or they are to blame for my addictions. No one is to blame besides us.

I used to play the blame game. I grew up in a large family, five boys and three girls, but I only grew up with one brother out of all the rest. He and I are only two years apart, me being older. All the other siblings were grown-ups. My younger brother and I grew up with our nieces and nephews. My oldest niece is six months older than myself, so you see, I have a large family. Now back to the blame game. I used to say that the reason I wound up on drugs was because my big brother, who returned from Vietnam when I was eight and my brother was six; he was to blame because he introduced us kids to weed. Bottom line, after we were old enough to know better, we should have made the decision or good choice not to do drugs; therefore, I cannot blame my big brother. I only have myself to blame. I now take full responsibility for my wrong choices that brought me to prison.

I'm ready to live out the rest of my years serving God and my fellow man. As I serve my God, I will also be serving my fellow man, and when I serve my fellow man, I will be serving God. When we live our lives with the humble spirit of God, we serve both God and man. So now, we know that service is the main thing, and it is better to serve than to be served. Now let us embrace sobriety within the bosom of our inner man, our spirit man, where we can be empowered by God's supernatural enlightenment and succeed in all we do in life, and let us renounce every evil and wicked thing in the flesh that causes conflict with our spirit man, our inner man. The spirit reigns over the flesh; therefore, we must always be willing to make the flesh submit to our higher spirit, in order that we may stay the course of our journey of sobriety, through the power of God and his spirit that dwells within us.

When we can bring our flesh under obedience to our superior spirits, we can spread our wings in the spiritual realm with a sense of peace and joy in the knowledge of knowing we have arrived to a pure truth about ourselves. Throughout the enlightenment of God, we see past the mind's eye of the natural man We are on the right track as it relates to our sobriety because we have learned to put our faith in God. We are growing daily and blossoming like beautiful flowers because we are trusting in God and recognizing our capabilities as well as our weaknesses. With our newfound spiritual selves, we find that we can be mature adults in every area of life where we can be free from addiction and silly individuals void of good sense and the knowledge of God because their lives are corrupt and filled with addiction, hate, jealousy, and deceit Therefore, we must dust our shoes off wherever we come in contact with these wicked and evil people. We must be careful not to let our spiritual guard down and succumb to the evils of drug and alcohol addictions and other evils.

I reiterate that real growth, as it relates to our sobriety, hinges on our spirituality. When we, as addicts, can allow God free rein in our lives, we will begin to grow in spiritual maturity and know oneness with God that will enable us to walk toward true spiritual sobriety one day, one step at a time. To allow God to guide our addicted, unmanageable lives, ultimately we will begin to feel a heavy burden lifted from us because we will no longer carry the burdens of the guilt, shame, and chaos associated with the lives of an addict.

We now rely on God's Holy Spirit to correct our lives and lead us in the path of righteousness where enlightenment and the knowledge of the truth lies. Our inner man, or our spirit, is at peace when guided by the Holy Spirit. The inner man, or spirit, is above and beyond the flesh; the spiritual man holds the keys to all that's good in this world and the next. The spiritual man makes things happen in the realest sense. He turns every dream into reality because the inner man is full of spiritual insight and enlightenment and purpose from God alone.

The spiritual man should live his life in the quest for true spiritual and daily sobriety, free from the insecurities of drugs and alcohol. When we let our spirit man lead us according to the will of God, our friends and environment will consist of people who are as drug- and alcohol-free as we are. Hopefully, as sober born-again Christians we can continue to grow spiritually, in order to further solidify our sobrietal condition to bring us to our ultimate spiritual maturity if at all possible. By God's grace, we should make every effort to achieve that level of sobriety and spiritual maturity because a mature sober Christian will love, respect, support, and protect himself, his family as well as others around him. Most of all, he will support other believers of God and worship Jehovah God with all his soul and being.

Only a true spiritual man can know peace and freedom from the clutches of drugs and alcohol. Through God's Holy Spirit, every willing soul can embrace real love, peace, prosperity, tranquility, and a serene existence with all mankind. With God in our lives, we can live our lives with full assurance of peace, sanity, and sobriety in bliss. Everything about us will take on a more livelier, fresher, and more exuberant face. Our lives, through God, are now much more than the mundane.

Remember, we are spiritual beings capable of great things because we see past the weakness of our mortal, limited flesh to transcend toward the heights of our immortality. We realize that we, through the spirit, are superior to our corruptible flesh. Our spirit man can successfully wage war against any and all addictions in life. Always be humble and even prayerful to Almighty God because he is greater than us and outside of us. God is eternal. He is the universal creator of all things, including us. Therefore, let us exalt our Maker with praise and count on him to sustain us and deliver us from our everyday storms because all things are possible with God, according to his Word.

It's up to us, though, whether we choose to follow and believe in his Word. It's high time we became connected and enlightened by his truth, in order that we can lay hold on the naked, absolute perfect truth, about the very nature of our problems in life. You see, only through surrender to our higher power, God, will we ever be able to unearth the exact nature of our addictions or problems in life.

All things will unfold when we surrender to God and ask for his help, direction, and forgiveness. When we do this, God will give us far more than we ever imagined or deserved.

God will prepare us to do battle against the devil and his addictions because there are going to be many times when Satan will attack us and try our determination to have sobriety. He will do it, for example, through the death of a loved one, the loss of companionship through divorce, etc. This is the time when Satan will tempt us with our addictions, but this is a perfect time to resist through God and stay the course of our sobriety.

Remember, the spirit man is stronger than the flesh. Though we are in the flesh, we must be led by the spirit Therefore, we have the power and authority through God to wage war against the evil wickedness of the devil's drugs and alcohol because we walk on a higher level of existence when we become one with Almighty God himself.

It is because of this that we are able to conquer the deceptive, abusive addictions thrown at us by the devil and his demons. We are God's chosen people, and as long as we allow him control over our lives, we will be all right. God is an ever-present help in time of trouble. Whatever the circumstance, we must realize that we are the temple of God, and we must be sure we keep it clean and free from the defilement of drugs and alcohol and every other sin and evil.

We are both spirit and flesh, but the spirit reigns supreme because our spirit is immortal—it never dies; whereas our weak flesh will die because it is mortal and born to see corruption. So we see that the spirit is our true essence and our flesh is only a temporary vessel born to die, yet it houses the real man, our spirit man. Therefore, we should never let our inferior flesh overrule our supreme and superior spirit man. From our very conception into our mother's womb, we were created as spiritual beings. Therefore, we need God's Holy Spirit to guide us through our every step in this life and the next.

God will give us added spiritual vision and a life of pure, unadulterated fulfillment on every level and in every area of life. We need to call on our spirit man and his real eyes to see past the carnal flesh whenever we feel the need to do so, in order that we can continue to bask in the glory of our peace, sobriety, sanity, and our spiritual victory over addictions as well. May we all relish in the joy that God would have all men to be saved and not perish in his sins. Therefore, we must persevere and press on daily with a sober mind, letting God guide our every step on our road of sobriety. God wants all the best for his children in this life and in the life eternal.

We must stop letting drugs and alcohol ruin our lives with the chaos, destruction, and confusion that they cause us in life because, surely, God is not the author of confusion.

Therefore, he would have us to live as a mirror reflection of his nature, and if we dare to do that, then we dare to live our lives in a state of order, sobriety, peace, love, and sanity. People, let's try our best to live our lives with humility, considering ourselves, yet even more, thinking about the needs of others.

When we can learn servitude and selflessness, we begin to tap to our spirit man where we are able to search the deep things, for we have spiritual discernment, and we see things that are higher than the flesh. The mortal flesh man can never understand the spiritual things because they are only for those of us who are spiritual. The natural man, in all his humanistic logic and rational glory, can never understand the things of the spirit because the spirit is unlimited and the flesh is frail and limited.

God is able to take the simple things in life and confound the so-called wise, or intellectuals, if you would, and even the men of so-called science who are noted for their secular scholarly brilliance. Man's wisdom, at best, is as filthy rags to God. Therefore, we must surrender to God and let him be our pilot in life. Yes, we must let God fly the airplane in our lives, unassisted by any copilot because God likes to do his thing solo. Remember, he needs no assistance; he only requires our prayers, faith, and trust in him.

God says in the Bible that his strength is made perfect in our weakness and that his grace is sufficient for thee. So, people, let's humble ourselves to our Almighty God and admit that we are weak and helpless without him; then he will give us his grace to strengthen us and make us strong enough to stand through life's ups and downs.

When we begin to allow God total access into our lives, his spirit will possess us, and we will have a changed heart and a changed spirit.

We will be one with the spirit of Almighty God, and we will no longer desire fleeting, sinful temptations in life. We will be more desirable of lasting treasures that will preserve our souls for eternity, and that lasting treasure is God's salvation, with which we can be assured of life everlasting. God's salvation will also give us power to war against the adverse temptations of this evil and wicked world we live in. With God's spirit inside of us, we can break the sinful yolks of addiction and bring back stability, sanity, peace, love, success, sobriety, and most of all, a restoration of our spiritual relationship with God the Father.

Our God is a God of sobriety, peace, love, sanity, order, power, and unconditional love for all mankind. Therefore, we should reflect these sane qualities by living like God. When we abandon drugs and alcohol in our lives, we will have taken the first step to a life full and rich with everything I've mentioned. As enlightened beings walking in the spirit of our Creator, we walk on a plane so much higher than the natural foolish man who will, because of his own humanistic logic and reasoning, spend a lifetime trying to be God unto himself or even convince himself that God doesn't exist even in the face of his very existence, being ironclad proof that God is.

Now we have this spiritual mind given us by God. We have the internal ability now to say no to addiction. I've often imagined what the world would be like without liquor stores and the influx of lucrative illegal drugs. Perhaps, the world in which we live, would be a more serene, sober, sane, orderly, loving, and more of a mirror reflection of a perfect, wholesome, God-fearing society, which God wants for all his children. This would be beautiful if it weren't for the ugly truth about the fact that reality in our world today is sickening.

Drugs and alcohol had reached epic proportions as it relates to sales and the people who are addicted—the people who have had their lives turned upside down, financially ruined, and living in a state of total confusion and utter chaos. You see, the reality of the ever presence of drugs and alcohol will continually be a thorn of temptation in the sides of every active addict and every recovering addict. The recovering addict's chance of successful sobriety or continuity, if you would, is far greater than that of the addict who willingly continues to use and who refuses to change and seek recovery through God. For only through God can we as addicts ever know what joy, peace, and recovery bring to our otherwise-unmanageable lives.

Change is extremely important to us, as addicts, if we truly want to enjoy the bliss of sobriety in recovery, and we also must be ever vigilant in our prayers and relationship to God that he may bless us with grace to endure this world of insatiable demonic temptations—drugs and alcohol being one of the chief temptations in the material world.

I recall, in my formative years of growing up, I had fantasies of being a pimp with a stable of hoes and a stone-cold gangster straight from the streets of ruthlessness. I mean, I wanted ice water to flow through my veins because I wanted nothing more than to be one of the hardest, most coldhearted gangsters in the game. Growing up, as a small boy, I was already involved in the criminal world, loosely speaking, the mob or the mafia. I was taught by straight killers how to shoot with precision various guns before I was of legal age. My favorite gun or strap was the 9mm Smith and Wesson. My favorite scatter gun was the Mossberg pistol-grip 12-gauge shotgun. My favorite assault rifles were the AK47, SKS, and the M16.

Yes, I was clearly consumed in the world of corruption. I was also taught how to sell and profit from the sales of cocaine and marijuana. Also, I learned all about the numbers game: high score tickets, tips, and parlay tickets for the ball games. Yes, I learned corruption and racketeering from some of, what I believed, were the best in the game.

These men were all hard-core, cold, straight gangsters, pimps, and killers who lived in my own neighborhood. They put plenty of trust in me. They allowed me to run business errands as I learned their business. I had the run of the household. I was treated like family. If ever trouble found me at that particular place, I would have been more than prepared. I had total access to an arsenal of weapons from civilian to military issue.

I learned quick how to multiply money, but evil wealth don't ever last. I went from what I thought was sugar to shit: from drug dealer to drug user. Seemingly overnight, I lost all my ill-gotten material possessions and became a crackhead who started to steal and rob to support my addiction.

My friends Skee-bop and G-man severed all ties with me as I continued to spiral downhill in my addiction, and finally I hit rock-bottom when I came to prison for aggravated robbery. My crack cocaine addiction was clearly out of control. Fact is, addiction of any kind is never controllable. My addiction brought me to prison where I reconnected with God, and through God and other people, God had already helped. I found peace and the strength and the good sense to realize that sobriety is the key to all peace and freedom on every level of life, while drug and alcohol addiction breeds criminal acts that will lead to imprisonment, death, hell, separation from family, and most importantly, a spiritual separation from God.

G-man and Skee-bop never, in the end, turned into geekies or addicts, but rather, what befell them was the ultimate punishment. They were charged and convicted as "drug kingpins." Now their lives will be spent in the federal pin. They will never get out or be able to spend time with their kids or other family in the free world ever again. Even though I went to prison as well, I went as a state prisoner to serve a minimal sentence with a chance to redeem myself and live within society as a productive citizen again. My friends, Skee-bop and G-man, have no chance at freedom's redemptive bliss ever again because they are doing federal prison life sentences.

My friend's lives of normalcy are over. Their feet will never touch free-world soil again. I am amongst the blessed ones whom God have chosen to show his mercy. Because of that I will live my life to the fullest without addictions and do all within my power to take my message to others what happened to me while I was drinking and drugging and that if others do as I did, then they will suffer the same chaotic plight or worse, death and hell. I pray that my message will bring a beacon of light and hope to the lives of others, that they may choose life and sobriety rather than death, chaos, torment, prison away from family, and ultimately, alienation from God.

Prison has brought great focus and insight into my life because I've had plenty of time to reflect on my past choices. Now I realize that I must be willing to change completely from the lifestyle I once led because that lifestyle brought me to prison in the first place. Also, I must renounce my past drinking and drugging; addiction only breeds destruction. Therefore, I decided to rearrange my life for the better. No more do I choose to drink and drug. No more do I choose unhealthy relationship. No more do I choose addictive friends. No more will I choose to hang out in my old environment where drugs and alcohol are readily available because all these things will bring me back to prison, destroy my life, my family, and my spiritual walk with God.

Clearly, it's better to serve God in sobriety and live in peace, sanity, and freedom rather than to serve the devil in addiction and lose family, freedom, my spiritual relationship with God, and finally, lose my own soul. There was a time, though, when I was caught between God and the devil. On the one hand, I knew what God would have me to do as a true Christian soldier. God would have every Christian to walk like Jesus and take *his* Word of salvation to the world and fish for lost souls. Then, on the other hand, I was in awe of all the worldly pleasures of the devil. Then, for a season, I served the devil, and I took sin with all the confusion and chaos that come with it to an all-time high. I didn't deny myself any abomination of sinful pleasures in life: drugs, alcohol, whores, money, gambling, and anything sinful that satisfied my desire. Even though I sinned against God, I still was relentless in serving him.

For a while, I was, indeed, the man of the hour, the man on the scene who proudly sold drugs and alcohol, robbed and cheated, gambled, and pimped whores for money—all in the name of my sinful addiction that I was never able to satisfy. You see, once I tasted the devil's poisonous drugs and alcohol, I knew then and there that it wouldn't be long before they destroyed me. Yet I proceeded and insisted on chasing that fleeting, temporary high that would mask my real problem for a moment.

All my constant drinking and drugging was always in vain because whenever I found myself sober again then I also found myself facing reality on a real, concrete basis. I needed to find a permanent solution to my addiction, and after asking for God to help me, I found peace, sanity, and sobriety on a daily basis. I found that the root of my addiction stemmed from my inability to admit to myself and to God that I had a problem. Now God is the pilot of my jet plane in my journey in life. I choose God to lead me in life because *he* will never fail me.

When I opened up my heart to God, I no longer let selfishness absorb my life. I began to realize that it is better to be selfless in nature and serve others rather than to be served and that my actions have consequences. Not only do my actions affect me but also the people I professed to love.

As I look back in retrospect at what my life used to be like in the dope game and the balling game where I did any and all I felt necessary to make that almighty green dollar, I often reflect at the many times when I'd have my girl to take photographs of me lying on my queen-size bed with a blanket of twenties, fifties, and hundreds underneath me. I'd also have her take pictures of me posing with different straps—which means different guns. But deep within me, I knew all this was wrong and sinful in the eyes of moral society and, most importantly, in the eyes of God.

Man, was I sick and obsessed with power and sinful, secular sins. As I look back in retrospect, I remember all the chaos and insanity that plagued my life when I was in the dope game and when I was a user of drugs and alcohol. When I was all grown-up, all the hard, ruthless hustle game was deeply rooted inside of my very soul. I tried hard to escape that part of me, but time after time it proved futile because I was a slave to the easy money, women, and power that the life of corruption gave me. No matter how I tried to change my life, sometimes hoping to lay hold on just a small portion of normalcy, that bitter taste of corruption loomed about me, ever present in my life, as if it were a part of my very being.

I even chose corruption as my career goal for a while in my life. All my friends that I grew up with were just like me, thugs and rogues at heart. We set out to establish our own private ranks in the game of crime. Man, did we ever "ball till ya fall," so to speak—meaning, we had plenty of yeo, (which is cocaine), and we made a mountain of cheese, which is money. Everything our hands touched turned money, green and gold. We had the Midas touch.

Today I'm drug- and alcohol-free with peace, sanity, and hope in my life, and I have no regrets for having given up that life. Even though I could have my girl take pictures of me lying down on my bed on top of piles of money—yes, underneath me and around me; my queen-size bed was a sea of mostly twenties, fifties, and hundreds—deep inside I knew all my money was evil because of the way I got it. Now I'm glad to be free of the demonic sickness that once ruled my life. No more do prestige, money, and power have a place in my life because I'm drug- and alcohol-free and living for a higher calling. That calling is my Lord and Savior Jesus Christ. It is by his mercy, grace, and favor that I am able to continue my walk of sobriety with confidence and hope one day at a time. I must be ever vigilant in my walk of sobriety, always remembering I'm always just a drink and drug away from using again. Also, I must always remember that trials may come and with them thoughts of guilt that can make one question or shake one's sobriety. Then, when this happens, we start to find reasons to relapse. Yes, we actually will make up excuses or, rather, rationalize our addictions as it relates to why we need that drink or drug of choice.

You see, I went through this when I had thoughts of guilt because of my cousin Sammy's death. I kept telling myself that I was the cause of his death. I would tell myself over and over again that if I hadn't sold him the tech 9 semi, he would still be alive today. But today I'm free from that guilt that helped me spiral into the chaotic abyss of substance abuse and alcoholism. I'm free in the sober assurance and knowledge through God that all things that have occurred or will occur are ordained by the will of God and not man.

Therefore, I have no more thoughts of committing suicide because of misplaced guilt. I'm now basking in the glory of my daily sobriety, yes, one day at a time. I will be glad and thank my God for the grace he has bestowed on my once-confused, addictive life. No longer is crack cocaine, alcohol, or a bullet to the head my choice as a means of suicide, whether, by means thereof, slow or fast.

I now approach every day with zest and thanksgiving, renewed in one of God's greatest gifts to man: sobriety. Yet daily and progressive as it is, I will stay the course by the grace of my God. Now I put all my evil vindictive thoughts behind me, for they breed hate and negativity. They even kill man's very soul. I've chosen forgiveness and positivity that my own soul may be saved as I join in a new life of daily progressive sobriety. I am refreshed and restored in my present state of sobriety, that through God's perfect merciful grace it will allow sobriety to give me focus in my life, that I may live it not in lack of anything, nor in chaos or confusion, but in abounding abundance.

All my childish reasons I once used to excuse away at justification for my addiction are now slipped away. No more blame or guilt because God is the Creator of all things; therefore, he is the reason for everything that occurs. God always knows the outcome of everything, yet at the same time, he gives us freedom of choice. God knew that I would end up in prison for aggravated robbery because of my addiction to drugs and alcohol but never chose this fate for me; he, rather, allowed it to happen of my own volition or choice. God knew that I would choose to commit the crime of aggravated robbery. He didn't make me do it; it was my own choice, but after it happened, I was utterly relieved of all the pain and suffering caused by my once-chaotic lifestyle where I never had a minute's rest in the street because of my voracious appetite for drugs and alcohol.

Prison gave me refuge and rest because I was no longer able to feed the beast. I finally was able to reconnect with God and normalcy. You see, prison gave me hope again and brought me to God's will to serve him in spirit and in truth with all humility and obedience through holiness, prayers, servitude to all mankind in resolute sobriety. In prison I learned to accept responsibility for my actions. I learned that every action had a consequence. I learned that every one of our actions or choices has consequences that affect us and the people around us, either positively or negatively. For life is about choices; therefore, it is extremely important for us to think long and hard before we act, and if we do this, we can make better choices in life that will prevent us from winding up in situations that alienate us from our families, such as jail time or prison time.

When we spend time in jail or prison, our families spend time there with us. While we suffer physically as well as psychologically and financially, our families suffer as well: psychologically, emotionally, and financially. As tragic as these things are, they do occur in many of our lives. It has happened in my life, but through it I've found redemption. God has forgiven me, I've forgiven me, and so has my family, which has given me the strength through God to learn on a daily basis how to fortify my walk of sobriety even in prison. Going to church services, 7 Steps, A. A., alternative-to-violence program, and the substance and alcohol programs will work if you are sincere in wanting them to help you.

I personally believe any program of substance and alcohol abuse, whether in prison or in the free world, is one inspired by Almighty God to redeem us and bring us back to his will of worship, holiness, servitude for each other, obedience, humility, and sanity in the walk or sobriety in our lives. As for me, I am ready to walk outside of the prison confines and worship my God in spirit and in truth, exercise full obedience to him, serve him as well as my fellow man, and obey the laws of God and man and live in a state of blissful sobriety and prosper in all abundance of life.

I can do all these things because of my faith in my God. My faith is in him because he is immortal and supreme, always strong and never weak. God has never let me down since I put my life in his hands and not the hands of man. For man is merely mortal, frail and weak, and man will forever let us down because their hearts are deceptive and they cannot be trusted by reason of their mortality. Therefore, I thank my God that he is a God of deliverance, salvation, and trust. Through the grace of God I will spend the rest of my days walking a daily progressive and even spiritual path in my sobriety. For God's grace and mercy will keep me from day to day along my lifelong journey to be ever sober and sane, glorifying in my God, for he is my ever-present help. Through God we can all find the strength to put drugs and alcohol behind us. When we truly love God and keep his commandments, we will begin to also love each other and serve each other with humility and obedience to God, and in doing these things we discover what the meaning of worshipping God in spirit and in truth really means. Through God we can summon his grace and find strength to make good decisions to guard us from the ravages of drug and alcohol abuse.

Through our own selfishness and lust we fall from grace into the abyss of addiction, and this bad decision leads to chaos and prison away from the people we love and that love us. Therefore, I choose a life of daily sobriety through spiritual perseverance. We must stay spiritually strong and allow God to pilot our lives because God is the only way we can hope to continue in our sobriety. God is our assurance of peace and joy where we can realize a sober, clean life as we bask in God's glorious gift of salvation where we become truly free in our inner man, because we are one with the universal power, God himself.

Because of our faith in our God, we are able to stand against the wiles of the devil's wicked devices of drugs and alcohol and find everlasting fulfillment in our lives of newfound sobriety. So we must remain ever vigilant and obedient to our God that we may continue on this beautiful path of sobriety that God has allowed us through his mercy to humbly walk.

Remember, we couldn't manage our own lives of chaotic addiction because of our frail, weak humanity. Therefore, we turned to an immortal everlasting power, God himself, for only God was able to bring us to sanity, sobriety, and order.

When all the devices of men shall fail, there will be the Bible then. It's God's Word of truth that will give us the spiritual strength to conquer secular sin, and if we follow God's perfect Word, we will come to the knowledge of the truth that every faithful believer is blessed by God, for we are the righteousness of God because we cast all our faith in him to protect us and deliver us through his grace, mercy, and favor. Therefore, with God's ever-present shield of righteous protection, we are able to war against the demons of drugs and alcohol and defeat them. We must remain diligent in our efforts to maintain our sobriety by letting God pilot the jet airplane in our lives. God and only God can bring victory to our lives to allow us to live drug- and alcohol-free and bring us complete peace and sanity on an everlasting basis.

God has given us a manual of instruction for our lives, and that manual is his Word, the Holy Bible. If we follow the manual, then we will find that it is the key to everything good in this life and the life to come. Yes, it is the supernatural Word of God that is able to accomplish all the things written therein for every believer who steps out in faith with God's Word as the number one thing in his life. Through God and *his* Word of truth, we lay hold on eternal peace of mind, body, and soul.

All things are possible with God, but man is weak and frail. Therefore, we have no hope in the flesh because the flesh will always fall short all alone. The flesh is too weak to battle the demons of drug and alcohol. If we abide in God's Word, we are made strong in the spirit, and we have hope and expectation for victory over every enemy through our great God, who nourishes all his children with spiritual food which is his Word, in order that we are made strong to battle all the infirmities of the flesh, and amongst the infirmities are the temptations of drugs and alcohol. God will never let us down as long as we never let him down by falling away from his manual for our lives, which is his Word of truth, the Bible.

Through spirituality we see the bigger picture. We realize the truth about addiction. We see that in the carnal, secular world in which we live, the drugs and alcohol will never disappear in our life-time, but with God's help we can resist the temptation to indulge in such an ungodly lifestyle. Through God we can be confident in our ability to maintain our own sobriety and bask in the glory of total peace and bliss.

Let us always be thankful to our God for delivering us from the hell of drugs and alcohol and the desire to sell drugs that has destroyed and devastated so many lives directly and even indirectly. Addiction creates hell on earth because it rips and tears away at the hearts of every addict as well as the addicts' families and other loved ones, and it causes financial disaster, loss of self-esteem, morality, birth defects, ghettos, homelessness, loss of freedom to a prison cell, and most of all, separation from our great God, who is able to save us from every sin.

God holds every one of us in the palm of his merciful and graceful hands, and he stands ready, willing, and able to reward those of us that are obedient to his Word. When we exercise obedience, God releases his blessings, then we can begin to live our lives for the better in the here and now because we are spiritually enlightened with the light of God's Word, enabling us to do all things even maintain our sobriety. For we have supernatural power through our great invisible God, who is the Creator of the universe.

God is all-powerful and will help those of us who ask for his help. He is knocking at the very heart and soul of mankind and is willing to save us all only if we let him in. We need to be willing to come to the knowledge of the truth about our inadequacies and the depth of our sins.

When we can do this, we can be saved and come to the knowledge of the truth about God's gift of grace that gives us salvation for eternal life. Today I've chosen to ask for God's grace, which gives us salvation and eternal life. Now I walk above my flesh, and now I walk on a spiritual path of sobriety while yet in my flesh because of God's great mercy and grace. It is my hope that all men would do as I have and experience God's mercy and grace which leads to salvation arid eternal life. You see, when we trust God for all these things, *he* will give us spiritual power where we are able to rise above the devil and his deceptive, sinful methods of temptations, like drugs and alcohol, and be ready to defeat him.

God said in his Word that no weapon formed against us shall prosper, but the devil and his demons and evil people that he uses will form these weapons against us because we are God's elect. God calls us in his Word a peculiar people, a royal priesthood; therefore, those weapons of the devil shall not prosper because of whom we belong to.

We are a strong, faithful, and spiritual people who realize that our battle is not carnal, which is to say the flesh, but rather, one that is spiritual. As the Bible tells us, God will always prevail over Satan and his demons and his human workers of iniquity. The spirit is strong and unlimited, but the flesh is weak and limited. Now, with all this knowledge, let us go forth on our journey of sobriety, giving thanks to our great God and the people like ourselves that he put in our lives to help us wage a victorious war against our addictions to drugs and alcohol. Let us also thank our great God for bringing us to the knowledge of the truth about our addictions that is the knowledge that we alone are not able to fight our addictions, but only through God's help are we able to tap into our God-given spiritual power and wage a successful fight or battle against the devil's drugs and alcohol.

People, we must always remember and never forget that man's programs for recovery is only a building block to our recovery and that true recovery rests in spirituality. God is of paramount importance because we are of weak mortal flesh and all our concepts and answers to our problems are but fleeting and temporary. When we trust in our invisible, strong, and immortal God, we begin to realize that he is our only answer for our addictions and all of life's problems because God is greater than ourselves and he is outside of us. God, and only God, is able to bring about everlasting, permanent solutions or answers to our problems of addictions and otherwise in life.

With God all things are truly possible; God said so in his Word, and he cannot lie.

Therefore, we must learn to be humble and obedient to God, and he will be our rock and refuge in time of need. Let us claim God's grace and mercy in our lives by stepping out in faith and admitting to ourselves that we are weak and powerless as it relates to controlling our addictions. When we are able to do this, God will show us mercy and grace. He will enable us to go forth strengthened by his own spirit toward our road of sobriety and recovery.

We will then realize that God is a God of real love, and we will begin to abandon self-pride and learn to embrace selflessness where we begin to serve our fellow man as God serves us. We begin to realize that it is better to serve than to be served, for this is the very nature of our great universal God. When we can finally realize that life is not all about self, then we begin to come to the knowledge of the truth that others factor into the equation of life as well and that all our decisions or choices in life affect others as well as ourselves, either directly or indirectly.

When we can start to import the aforementioned principles into our lives, we will see marked improvement in our overall lives. We will find sanity, sobriety, and a peaceful bliss such as we have never known. We see the world with renewed wisdom. We see past our flesh. We have spiritual enlightenment by the grace and mercy of God, and we have the power to see the truth about drugs and alcohol as it relates to the devastation, destruction, and every evil detrimental thing they cause in lives of mankind. Because we are empowered within by God, we are able to walk that path of sobriety on a daily and progressive basis. Through God we can be consummate champions over drug and alcohol addiction and rest in the knowledge that we can remain free from the bondage of addiction as long as we abandon all hope for help from our own weak, limited flesh and rely on God to strengthen our spirit with his own strong, unlimited spirit. We must cast all our faith and trust in God, in order that he can build us up daily with the spirit of humility, obedience, and a spirit of total trust in our loving, powerful, and compassionate God. When we submit to God and allow him free rein in our lives, he will reward us and lift us up from every low place in life. Now, may we, through the power of God's empowering spirit, strive on toward our path of sobriety for lifelong sobriety. God is able to transform our lives for good as long as we give him access by asking for his help.

God cannot be moved or shaken; he is our solid, unmovable rock of refuge who remains unchanged and stable. His place and being cannot be disrupted. He is our hope and our salvation for eternal life. Therefore, let us be glad and ever thankful to God and press on with humility and obedience to him as we endeavor to walk our path of sobriety, forever strengthened in our spirit by our total faith in our God, because hope in God is the key to change for the better in all things in this life and the life eternal. Now let us walk the path of true spiritual sobriety, which is the only path whereby we can overcome the weak flesh. True spiritual sobriety is when we rely on God's own spirit to empower our very spirits with strength to enable us to do all things according to his mercy and grace, including beating our addictions to drugs and alcohol. For only God can and will do for us what we, in our flesh, couldn't do for ourselves as it relates to our addictions. With God at the helm of our lives, we will have control and victory in our lives over all our addictions in life, and we will reap the harvest of good in abundance when we give God free rein in our lives and abandon the chaotic, destructive life of drugs and alcohol.

Always remember too: God helps those of us who choose to help themselves. If we take one step, God will surely take two. I know all of us have heard these comforting words before, but we must be more than hearers; we must be true believers of these words. Remember, God's Word tells us to be believers of his Word and not just learners and that faith without works is dead. So we must all walk as true believers in God's Word, having no doubt he will accomplish in us everything he promised. Only then will we start to reap the fruits of our belief for our actions of faith, for *faith* is an action word, and we must act on it.

Therefore, we must put our faith in action and stand strong together and fight any and all adversity in our lives that causes us harm and detriment. With faith we can have victory over every obstacle in our lives, including drugs and alcohol. We must remain ever vigilant in our quest to defeat the dark powers of alcohol and drugs. Through Christ we have the power to utilize our faith to conquer the devil and his devices of secular sin. Faith is of paramount importance as it relates to our success in sobriety. We can achieve if we believe.

Whatever we need we must name it and then take action and know through faith in God we can claim it. You see, this is God's unfailing formula of faith. With all that in mind, we now have full assurance of the fact that our God wants us to be happy by depending on him to supply our every need in life. Whenever we exercise our faith, we show trust and obedience to our God. He will then reward us for having had faith and trust in him and for being obedient to his will for our lives, which consist of every good thing imaginable.

Now let us walk in the light of faith and come out of the darkness of death, that we may cause our brothers and sisters to be encouraged and strengthened spiritually by our assurance in our faith so that they may show others this gift of light called faith and cause a domino effect for the good of all mankind, giving hope for a future of sobriety, peace, sanity, and a true personal relationship with our great God.

As for me, I walk in the gift of light called faith every day of my life because I know my God is real and he rewards those of us who has faith in him. Therefore, with daily diligence, I feed my soul with the nourishment of God's food that I may increase my faith and grow stronger in the spirit, that I may successfully defeat the strongholds of drug and alcohol addiction in my life and find the blissfulness of sobriety, peace, sanity, and reverence to God, which is the will of God.

When we can humble ourselves to our God and be obedient to his will in our lives, we can rest certain that God will strengthen our spirit and enable us to walk a daily and progressive path of sobriety. Those of us who are strong in spirit should bear the burdens of our weak brothers and sisters who are weaker than us because they rely on man, which is but carnal flesh, for solutions to their drug and alcohol addictions, rather than on our strong, invisible, spiritual God who is able to do all things for our good.

Now, with a pure heart, let us go forth with the tools of faith and love and make straight the path of sobriety for our brothers and sisters. May we, as touching and agreeing in faith as fellow brothers and sisters, strive for daily progressive sobriety, learning to serve each other as it relates to taking care of one another's needs. After all, Jesus, our Lord, serves us, and he was, indeed, our master. Therefore, the servant isn't greater than his master, so we should with great reverence to our Lord take on the nature of a servant to our fellow brothers and sisters because in doing so, we reflect the very nature of our God.

When we serve one another, then we serve God himself. When we can live our lives like Christ, we can walk our path of sobriety with complete assurance because God will accomplish good in the lives of all those who will serve him with complete and pure love, faith, and obedience. Though the devil will lay snares and devices in the path of every sober spiritual soldier, he will not prevail. Because God is our enabler, he has given us power spiritually over all evil—whether the carnal, secular devices of the devil called drugs and alcohol, or spiritual weapons by the devil designed to wound and destroy one's soul.

The devil, who is the spiritual leader of the angels and demons of darkness who work in the children of disobedience, will form weapons against all of God's children because that is his very sin and evil nature. We, through the spiritual power of our God, are now renewed and refreshed, and we see through the real eyes of spiritual enlightenment, which gives us power over the devil and his workers of iniquity that seek to steal our souls. Now, having a true faith in our God and being empowered by his spirit, we have the spirit which is his to crucify daily the carnal, secular sin that so casually besets us that we may reveal our true spirit nature that transcends all flesh, for truly in spirit we are the righteousness of God. Therefore, we must walk in righteousness and forsake the unrighteousness of all willful sins in our lives, such as drugs and alcohol.

If we walk in righteousness, our every trial and tribulation will get easier to bear because our spiritual righteousness will convict us and we will inherently want to do the right thing, the righteous thing. The spirit of God is powerful and those of us who has his spirit can never be limited by man who is but weak flesh. We, through the power of our God, can do all things, for we are of God's own spirit and we rely not on the natural things of the flesh but we look to and rely on the things of God, which are unlimited, all-powerful, and spiritual.

You see, man, in his natural human state, always looks for answers to everything the form a rational, logical, and simple humanistic viewpoint. All because he can never comprehend the things of the spirit because it's too high for his natural mind to understand, so he dismisses it as foolishness. We, who have tasted of God's enlightening spirit, can see the answers to the deep things because we are spiritual. We have the spirit of God himself working within us.

Therefore, we have the discernment of our God to see past the flesh to the spiritual things of our God. We as empowered spiritual people should encourage our weak brothers and sisters who still rely on their own flesh to enable them and to help them solve problems, such as drug and alcohol addictions in life. We should show them that God and God alone is the only way to ever truly walk the path of sobriety and know God's peace again. Man in his flesh, at best, only provides for temporary fleeting solutions to mammoth problems that can only be resolved through the power of God himself. Therefore, we must let our brothers and sisters know that for God to help them, they must abandon all self-pride, be humble, have faith, and give God free rein to pilot their life. If and when they do this, they can begin to walk with confidence the path of daily progressive sobriety strengthened by the gift of God and *his* inner spiritual light that gives *his* strength and direction along our journey of sobriety.

I will count it all joy if I can save the life of just one addict by showing him or her just how God saved my life, when I asked him through faith and humility and by giving God free rein to pilot my life, according to his good will. You see, God, and God alone, can change the natural state of our fleshly reliant minds and replace it with the supernatural state of the spirit because when God gives us the gift of the spirit, we begin to see with real eyes—yes, true enlightened eyes of the spirit, which surpass the limited bounds of human flesh.

Through the gift of our great God, we truly walk in the flesh but are led by God's own spirit that dwells and works within us, and that same spirit should shine forth to our weaker brothers and sisters who are led by the flesh so it may convict them of the knowledge of the truth and open their eyes to the gift of the spirit of God, which is a beacon of hope for all mankind. If we live with this hope, we can stay the course of our sobriety.

With God at the helm of our sober lives, we can all maintain our sobriety and champion every obstacle Satan puts before us as it relates to addictive drugs and alcohol. Be ever sure, though, that there will be many times of trials and tribulations where we will be tempted by our addictions. God said that with every temptation, he will make a way to escape the temptation. Therefore, we should be obedient to our spirit and not give place to our own fleshly lust.

Now, because we are still human beings who aren't perfect, we will make mistakes that will cause us to fall sometimes, but God said if we ask his forgiveness, we will be forgiven. He said that he would, and God cannot lie. Although he forgives us of our sins, our sins are not without consequences, which means that God will chastise us because we were disobedient. Because we are his and his spirit dwells and walks within us, we are given many chances to get back into God's will.

God loves his children unconditionally. God is a God of great mercy, grace, love, forgiveness, and salvation. He is, also, a God of wrath, destruction, and vengeance. He doesn't like to be tempted or mocked, and he said that there remains no more sacrifice if we sin willfully. Therefore, let's come together in unity and sobriety in the power and spirit of our God that we may conquer the devil's demonic addictions of alcohol and drugs in our lives. We should also live in the knowledge of the truth about the sobriety, bliss, sanity, peace, and love God has for his faithful and obedient children.

In the spirit of God's will for good in our lives, let us go forth in the spirit of sobriety and walk the path of our sobriety with confidence that, through God, we will be able to stay our course, even lifelong, to the obedience of our God. Now, we must all remember that sobriety is the prize we strive for as it relates to the rest of our days. It won't be easy as it is a constant battle between the devil's demons and his children of disobedience who work against us through our addictions to alcohol and drugs. Therefore, we must be alert and be warned of wolves in sheep's clothing who seek to destroy our sobriety and even our very own souls. They would, if at all possible, deceive the very elect of God because they are cunning craftsmen in their evil. Then, while having a form of godliness, they deny the power thereof, and the Word of God said from such turn away. Satan always comes to us when we least expect him, looking to prey on our weaknesses—yes, our vulnerabilities, such as our addictions to drugs and alcohol—which leads to destruction, crime, prison, where we are separated from the people we love and the people that love us. We lose our freedom to the privileges of the free world, and we fall from the grace and will of our God.

Therefore, as spiritual and sober people, it is our duty to take our message of sobriety and hope to our fellow man who still struggles with addiction, hoping that it will shine forth as a beacon of everlasting light to enable them to come to the knowledge of the truth that God is able to help them overcome their every addiction in life. He will give them the peace, bliss, sobriety, sanity, and most of all, a renewed spirit just as he has given us through his mercy and grace.

Therefore, let us all come together walking in faith and obedience to God that we may know his perfect will for all good things for our lives. So now we must abandon selfish pride, and let us become selfless servants to each other, and in doing this we, indeed, serve our God. When we are able to do all these things with every ounce of our mortal and spiritual being, we then begin to see God's favor shower down on us in our lives. God will give us purpose and direction in our lives. When we let God rein in our lives, we will be able to walk our path of sobriety on a true daily and even spiritually aided basis because God enables our spirits to do what our weak flesh cannot.

Therefore, we know we have power over our weak flesh and that we, through the spiritual power of God, can overcome every addiction in our lives, including drugs and alcohol. Through God we have strength to do all things. We may live and walk in our fleshly bodies, but we are led by an immortal invisible spirit who is God himself, who quickens us with the power of his own spirit so that we can utilize his spirit that dwells and works within us to war a spiritual warfare over our fleshly addictions, thereby making our weak addiction to alcohol and drugs but a fleeting memory.

As we grow in God's Word and walk in the path of his promise of complete salvation in our lives, we begin to realize that God is a merciful, graceful, and all loving God and he will never let us down. As we continue in faith and obedience to his will, we will start to see clearer every day with a more progressive vision as it relates to God's will for the goodness of sobriety, peace, sanity, bliss, and most importantly, a renewed spirit between us and our God.

When we can at last lay hold on such a relationship, we will find an abundance of grace and mercy waiting for us in the palm of God's open hands all for our taking. Among the many gifts of God's treasures of mercy and grace are spirituality, sobriety, sanity, peace, and total bliss. If we remain steadfast in our pursuit to walk our daily progressive path of sobriety aided by spirituality, shed forth on us to utilize for strength to overcome all weaknesses of the flesh by God, including the carnal weaknesses of our addictions of drugs and alcohol that destroy and devastate many of our lives. When we unite in the spirit of faith with our God in front of us against the enemy of the devil's deceptive addictions of drugs and alcohol, we will have victory over this weakness because we are one in the spirit of the immortal invisible spirit who is God himself.

Nothing of the flesh can ever defeat him or those of us who have his spirit inside of us and that is working actively within us. Remember, the spirit is all-powerful and the flesh is frail and weak. Therefore, my faith is in my God to enable me daily with his own spirit that it may continue to live and work within me, that I my remain sober. My hope is in our merciful and graceful God because he will never leave or forsake us. I am among men most blessed because God has given me hope for a sober today, and I am ever thankful for today in my sobriety as it is truly a gift from my God.

For I have nothing in tomorrow or the future to speak of but an ever-abiding hope that is God willing that I live then with his help. I will, by *his* grace, still choose to be sober and clean. God is my hope in all I do. *He* is my guide on my ever-progressive daily journey of sobriety throughout the rest of my life in this world of sinful temptations. God can be the hope in every one of our lives if we humbly ask him. We cannot transform our lives of addiction now or later because it is now impossible for us, and later on it will still be the more impossible for us. Only with the help of God himself can we ever realize true transformation of our addictive lives.

God can bring us to the knowledge of the truth about our problems of addiction. They open our eyes of spiritual enlightenment in order that we stay the course of our sobriety. When we take off our fleshly blindfolds that blind our inner true spiritual vision, we can have confidence in the continuity of our sobriety. We—as renewed, enlightened, sober, and spiritual people—should relinquish and abandon all hope in the secular, sinful material world. We must realize that it is the power of God and God alone that will restore our once-addictive, chaotic lives back to sobriety and sanity and help us to regain fellowship with our family, friends, community, and most of all, abiding personal fellowship with our God.

God never intended that mankind live in chaos and confusion because of addictive drugs and alcohol that is one of the chief detriments to a would-be sober and sane life. Though we walk in the flesh, we, who seek God's favor, should rather be led by his spirit that we may lay hold on sobriety and the good on every level of life, which is what God wants for every one of us.

Therefore, we must be led by the spirit, in order that we reap every good gift from God. When we come to the knowledge of the truth of what the grace of God can do in our lives, we will then learn to submit to God with total humility and all due reverence to God's grace, mercy, and incomparable power that enables us to stand firm and stay the course of our sobriety.

We have an assured hope as it relates to our journey of sobriety because Jesus Christ gave us that hope when he died on the cross at cavalry, then went on later after a while to ascend into the heights of heaven to sit down on the right hand of the Father. So, having said this, we have absolutely no reason to fail at anything we aspire to in life because Jesus gave us eternal hope, and with such hope we can do all things, including remain sober and clean as it relates to drug and alcohol addiction. If we cast all our cares to God, then he will give us hope to live every day in a state of positivity, for positivity breeds success on every level of life. We can realize a sober, sane, peaceful, blissful, and most importantly, a renewed spiritual life where God is the center of our lives.

Through God and his graceful gifts, we can make real our every dream. We can truly have the "big house," "big yard," "white picket fence," "two or three vehicles," "big bank account," "a few kids," "a pet," and most importantly, a Christian wife who is God-fearing and loyal. For me, this would be my American dream. Whatever our dreams may be, we can realize them if we stand on the assured hope of our God. Now let us come together and rest in the mighty hope of our God, who is outside of us and greater than us. For "God is the Universal King." His power is unlimited. He is all-knowing, everywhere all the time, all-seeing, self-created, self-existent, without beginning, without ending, from eternity past. God is just what he is, and there are no other gods besides our God, Jehovah.

With God on our side, we have sure victory over any and all of life's problems, even those of drug and alcohol addiction. When we realize this, we can be ever vigilant in our walk of sobriety through the enabling, graceful hope bestowed upon us by our loving God. We know that the weak flesh is prone to a multitude of sins, but we also know that if we are led by God's spirit that dwells within us, then we can bear the sinful temptations of the flesh and stand firm in the assured hope of our God and remain sober and vigilant as we press on for that prize of eternal sobriety. Let us, therefore, walk in the power of God's unrelenting spirit, for that same spirit is able to do the supernatural, and this very spirit dwells in all of God's children.

So if you hear his voice, then you are his child, and you can accomplish the supernatural works of God himself, for his spirit that is within man compels you to do his will. We know his will is to do good. When we tap into this God spirit within, we then are able to successfully wage war with the carnal world of sin, where Satan, his demons, and the children of disobedience rule. Yes, we have power through God to overcome this world of carnal sin, where Satan reigns. We can even overcome addictive drugs and alcohol, which is amongst Satan's number one arsenal of deception designed to destroy the lives of all who fall prey.

Let us be warned and keep our faith and hope in God through total submission to him, that we may witness God's authority and power in our lives as he removes every form of carnal sin from our lives, even that of drug and alcohol addiction. This will allow us freedom from the clutches of Satan himself, that we may live sober, sane, blissful, peaceful, and righteously upon the precepts of God himself. We must surround ourselves with other God-filled believers such as ourselves in order that we may help one another as it relates to encouraging one another to stay the course of sobriety, that we may fulfill the very goodwill of God who dwells within us. When we do all this, then we begin to grow and blossom and bring forth the fruit of enlightenment that opens our eyes to a spiritual awakening, that we may clearly and with all newness see for the first time with the real eyes of the spirit the ugly truth about our weak, ungodly addictions to drugs and alcohol. The fog and haze are now lifted, and that old blind man can see now. He is no more in the darkness of a drug and alcohol induced haze. Now we see with true light—yes, through spiritual eyes, we can see past all adversity that we may overcome the sinful, deceptive addictive drugs and alcohol that once enslaved us.

We are now free and able to proceed toward a life of sobriety, sanity, bliss, peace, and most importantly, we can worship our God in spirit and in truth, having come to the knowledge of the truth that God wants us to be sober and diligent as we fulfill our life's destiny that God has for us. Bear in mind, though, God doesn't force us to accept or to do anything in life. We must choose to allow God to help us. Yes, it must be of our own volition in accepting his help or, rather, in asking for his help. We must be sincere and obedient. Therefore, we must walk in total conviction of the spirit and completely abandon self and give way to total absolute submission to God's divine power that is above and beyond the flesh. With that divine power, we can be assured of God's ever-present help that will enable us to defeat addictions to drugs and alcohol. God will also enable us to bring others to the knowledge of the truth, that they may experience the same blessed hope that we have experienced, that they may overcome drugs and alcohol addiction just as we have. Now, with all this said, let us all come together with the same mind that we may seek only pure things and things that reflect the nature of our loving, merciful, and graceful God.

When we are able to do this, then all thoughts of selfishness, pride, and unrighteousness will naturally slip away. The old thoughts will be replaced with the new thoughts of humility, sobriety, righteousness, and a true inner desire to serve our fellow man. In doing so, we serve God himself. When we begin to trust God for everything in our lives, we will lose all fear of what people or circumstances can do to us, for we have full assurance through our God that he will always protect and provide for our every need. We are his sheep, his children, and he is our Shepherd, our Father, and our God. Because we are God's elect, we walk on a plane of higher existence where we are led by the spirit of God that dwells within us, and by his abundant grace and mercy, we are able to find our purpose in life.

With true enlightenment of our spirits, we will be able to continue on in our journey of sobriety. God has given us new freedom. We are no longer enslaved by the devil's devastating drugs that once destroyed our lives. Now, our lives are filled with hope and are far more than the mundane. Every waking moment is one of beauty, and life is truly good and has great meaning.

Now, as free children of God, let us celebrate our lives with obedience to our God as we worship him in spirit and in truth and live every day in the glory of blessed sobriety. We must always remember never to trust in our weak flesh and blood because our power is limited at best. God is spirit and strong, and his power is unlimited. Therefore, we should cast our worries, fears, troubles, problems, and whatever seems to be bothering us right at the feet of our God, for he never fails because he is the "Supernatural Supreme Universal King."

We have failed in our own attempts to solve our problems of addiction many times. Yes, all our efforts where to no avail. Now, I say, we should try something outside of ourselves and something greater than ourselves. This *something* is Almighty God himself. God is able to do all things if we are able to believe that *he* can and then *he* will. You see, God wants us to have faith in him; therefore, we must admit to ourselves, others, and most importantly, to God himself that we have a need or a problem in our lives that can only be resolved by his mercy and grace. That's when God will intervene and strengthen us with his spirit, and then we will be empowered to do battle in this secular world filled with its many sinful, tempting vices.

Through the spirit of God that now dwells within us, we can resist any and all secular, sinful temptation. We see past our weak flesh. We have come to the knowledge of the truth through our God and have a new sight—that sight being a spiritual sight where we see the bigger picture as it relates to God's will for our lives. God would have all men to come to the knowledge of the truth and be saved and live in sobriety where we find bliss, peace, and most importantly, a renewed spiritual relationship with our God. We can have these things if we believe them. We can achieve. You see, faith is of paramount importance. It is the key to abundant treasure and blessings of our God, and if we are to reap these treasures and blessings, we must have faith in God.

If we have faith in God we must exercise it. We must rebuke everything and everybody who would oppose God. We must be holy, for God is holy. We must renounce the sins of the world and live for God in obedience and worship him in spirit and in truth in "holiness and sobriety." When we do these things, we will find favor with our God because of our obedience. As long as we continue in our obedience to God, he will continue to bless our lives with his treasures and blessings. Now, remember this too: God helps those who help themselves. So we should step out in faith every day believing that God can and will supply all our needs and deliver us from all our sinful vices no matter what they are. With all this being said, then by faith we know we can walk a path of sobriety and reap God's bountiful blessings and abundant treasures and find a completeness of mind, body, and soul, where we bask in total peace, bliss, and a spiritual oneness with our God.

Now, we mustn't forget that we walk in the flesh, which is full of sin nature, but we should, rather, through the power of our God, be led by the spirit of God that dwells and lives in us, as his faithful obedient children. We know that in the flesh we shall be faced with a multitude of trials and tribulations in this sinful, secular world. We can overcome all sinful adversities when we give way to the God spirit that dwells and lives within us. We must be obedient to our inner man because he sees past our weak mortal flesh with real eyes—yes, the eyes of the spirit. The spirit man convicts us to the glory of the knowledge of truth, and that is God's will for our lives.

God is our only hope for all good things in this world and the next. Through our God, we are able to live in a state of blissful sobriety where we can encourage each other along our journey toward everlasting sobriety. When we give our God complete rein in our lives, our spiritual eyes are opened and we are enlightened to the knowledge of the truth about all the good things God wants for us. We can have them if we give him free rein. We can do this by repenting of our sins and worshipping God in spirit and in truth. We must, indeed, turn from the very sins and addictions that make us slaves to this world and Satan himself.

We must learn to walk in sobriety where we can see clearly and think clearly, yes indeed. We must be led by the spirit of God that dwells and lives in each of us and abandon and overcome our weak mortal flesh that we walk in every day because it is contrary to our godly spirit, which is superior and immortal. Sobriety is obedience to our God, and it begins when we admit to our higher power, whom I choose to call God, that we are powerless over our addictions and sins in our lives and that we need God to restore order, peace, sanity, bliss, and most of all, we need *him* to restore our spiritual relationship with *him*. Where good judgment and sobriety reign, chaos and confusion can rule no longer.

God is the foundation of every good and pure accomplishment in life. Therefore, it would behoove us all to build our lives up on the strong meat of God's Word and with earnest faith in God that we can receive the fruits of God's abundant treasures and plentiful blessings that he is ready to bestow upon the lives of those of us who will obey him. I'm sure, by now, many of you, readers, would maintain that I have been pretty repetitious in some of the things I've written as it relates to drug and alcohol addiction and the chaotic destruction and devastation it has caused and will cause for every one of us who love and continue to use them.

Don't be alarmed at all by my repetitiveness because I'm repetitive for a serious reason: the reason being that I want to emphatically stress just how devastating and destructive drug and alcohol abuse is and how it will ruin everything we ever held near and dear to us, whether it be material possessions, respect for self and others, your family and friends, your freedom, your peace, your sanity, your sobriety, and finally and most importantly, drug and alcohol addiction will separate us spiritually from our God and ultimately destroy our very souls. Now let us ponder about this and ask ourselves the million-dollar question: What is an alcoholic and an addict? Well, let me be as frank and candid as I know how with you in answering this so-called million-dollar question that has eluded many of us for years. My take on the matter is this: Anyone who has lost the ability to have a drink is a drunk or an alcoholic, and he or she also lacks the reasoning or rationale needed to separate business from pleasure; or quite simply, they cannot shut down the party, and the same holds true for the drug addict. The alcoholics and drug addicts are disasters waiting to happen because they have no self-control.

They suffer from grave living problems. They seek an escape from their living problems, as temporary as it may be, when they choose to self-medicate themselves with drugs and alcohol in hopes of making their sick, addictive living problems go away as long as possible. We all know when the party is over and reality sets in, that the same problems are ever present and are ever still dangerous. More often than not, it takes a real tragedy to strike before the party for the alcoholic and addict is ever brought to an end. Now that I've answered the age-old million-dollar question of what an alcoholic and an addict is to the best of my knowledge, I want all of you, readers, to look deep inside of your heart of hearts and let your inner man, which is the God spirit that dwells and lives inside of you, to tell you if I speak the truth according to your own spirits.

My opinion is that we will be in full agreement and our spirits will be on one accord in what we've discerned as it relates to the question already aforementioned. Since we believe on one accord, let us proceed on ever diligent and ever vigilant as we journey toward our path of sobriety using our spirit man to empower us that we may stay the course of our path of sobriety. Now let us abandon drugs and alcohol that only lead to death and hell and let God lead us to eternal bliss and peace by giving us his spirit that will enable us to find grace and sobriety to lead us to the bosom of God himself.

We must surrender all to God and let him be our beacon of hope and our eternal everlasting guide in this world and the next because he is worthy, for he is the Universal King. God is the Creator of all things in heaven and in earth. I write and dedicate this manual about the devastation and chaos that drugs and alcohol caused in my life in hopes that I may help fellow brothers and sisters who have suffered from the same problems and the many that still suffer in hopes that I may enlighten them as it relates to the feet that there is hope; I've found it through the grace of God. Therefore, they can find the same power as I have to turn away from the ravages of drugs and alcohol and taste the sweetness of the mercy and grace of Almighty God himself as he begins to transform their lives from the slave chains of the devil's drugs and alcohol to lives of liberty. This is where sobriety, sanity, peace, bliss, and spiritual renewal await us.

I've caused a lot of heartache and grief to my loved ones and others as I glorified drugs and alcohol. Now I can truly say that I'm sorry for breaking the laws of society and, most importantly, for disappointing my God. Hindsight is always twenty-twenty, and what's done is done; it's the past. I now live in the present. I look to what is before me. God has forgiven me of all my past wrong choices as it relates to breaking the laws of God and man. God has made me whole. I no longer want or need drugs and alcohol in my life. I no longer live for the fleeting secular pleasures of crack cocaine and the liquor bottle. I live now for the permanent, everlasting pleasures found in the simplest things in life, such as having dinner with my family, a picnic, going to church, praying and writing poetry, and so forth.

You see, these things are pure and wholesome things that can lead us to a complete spiritually clean and healthy life. With faith in our God, we are able to defeat every vice and live our lives in total sobriety where we can achieve realistic goals. So I say, let's all go ahead and dream the dream of hope. That dream starts with sobriety.

Sobriety is possible only if we are willing to submit to God by giving him free rein in our lives and allowing him to correct our sick living problems as it relates to our addictions to drugs and alcohol. We couldn't control our unmanageable lives of drug and alcohol addiction as our every attempt and effort proved futile. Therefore, we must surrender to God with the knowledge that he is able to do for us what we couldn't do for ourselves as it relates to the control of our addictions to drugs and alcohol. We must relinquish all selfishness, pride, and the attitude of "I can help myself" when we know that we cannot.

Therefore, we must, with complete humility and total abandon of self-will, let God's absolute power transform our addictive lives for the better. God can and will help us if we let him. He is knocking at the door of every human heart, and he will only come in to us if we open our heart's door. Indeed, we must be willing to change and put our past bad choices that caused us to lose control of our lives and fall prey to addiction's insanity far behind us. Nevertheless, we must also, even still, reflect on the bad choices we made in our past that led us to our unmanageable, chaotic addictions.

We must never dwell, as it will stagnate or slow down our progress of sobriety, and if we allow this to happen, we won't be able to build on a positive change for the future of good sobriety. Therefore, we must oppose the negativity of our past bad choices and pursue the good that positive sobriety can offer us. Now I say that we all must be willing to change from the negativity of our past bad choices that can lead to destruction, chaos, loss of freedom to a prison cell away from the people we love and that love us as well. Indeed, we must oppose this type of negativity and make a conscious choice to change for the positivity of the good life sobriety can bring: a life of sanity, order, peace, and most importantly, spiritual renewal with Almighty God and complete freedom on every level of life. Let us put the mistakes of yesterday far behind us and renew and refresh ourselves with the positivity of change. If we dare to change our lives, then we can become a sure beacon of hope for ourselves and others. If we say no to change, then we say yes to failure, chaos, destruction, drug and alcohol addiction, loss of our freedom to a prison cell away from the people we love and that love us as well, and most importantly, we will suffer separation from our loving God.

Therefore, we must embrace change as our absolute and only real vehicle that can ensure us a life of sobriety, peace, sanity, prosperity, freedom, and most importantly, it will ensure us a spiritual personal relationship with our God. Without God change would never be possible. So now we see that change is truly the key to every good thing in this life and in the life eternal to come. God wants us all to be a party to positive change, as it is the seed of the good life where we live life more abundantly on every level of life. As I press on and live my life daily in the state of sobriety, I now realize the importance of sobriety, family, freedom, and most importantly, a spiritual relationship with my God. I know now that all these things are far too precious to give up because of selfish, bad choices to drugs and alcohol that cloud one's reasoning and judgment, ultimately leading one to commit selfish acts of crime that cause one to fall prey to imprisonment away from family and friends, and most importantly, it causes one's spiritual separation from one's loving God.

Without God in one's life, we are doomed to fail at everything we pursue in live, including our sobriety. Therefore, we must make a change in our lives where God is at the helm of our every decision. If we make this godly change, then sobriety is truly possible for us all.

Now we all can discover hope for life.

TESTIMONIALS

From people who have suffered the ravages of drugs and alcohol addiction and how it took God himself to enable them and also myself to overcome the addiction and realize the goodness and sensibility of sobriety.

My own personal testimony

I WAS DELIVERED FROM A self-imposed prison of the mind and spirit. I was set free from the demonic and horrific clutches of drugs and alcohol by learning to trust and depend on an all-powerful, all-knowing, all-compassionate God, who is able to save us to the uttermost. I admitted to God that I couldn't manage my own life and that I would continue on a path of chaos and destruction unless he allowed his mercy and grace to touch my life and save me from hell and the grave.

I asked for God's intervention, and he gave ear and helped me. God is able to do all things because he is a spiritual, supernatural, supreme being who is not of the mortal, weak, dying flesh but of a self-created and self-existent eternal nature—a Supreme God of the Universe. He far surpasses man's limited intellect. Therefore, after I admitted my weakness and inability to control my problems in life with drugs and alcohol. I cast my complete trust in God with complete abandon to self-pride. I began to trust God for every need and not depend on other people or self.

Man sometimes will let us down, but God never does. God is a consummate winner. Therefore, I have total trust in God's ability to change and transform my addictive life for the better. With reverence, humility, and total selflessness, I began to realize that it's not all about self in this world; other people factor into the equation of life as well. Therefore, servitude to others is necessary and also service and reverence to God himself. So I'm giving myself to others and God. I've learned, with God's mercy and grace, to deal with many adversities in prison.

Amongst some of the things I learned are the following: people who engage in various taboos of nature, society, chronic liars, violence, misplaced anger, people who wear two faces, and people who just constantly keep making the same bad old choices and decisions.

Despite the unpleasantness of prison and the harsh reality of being in prison, I've learned responsibility and discipline. Yes, I've truly grown and blossomed into the full maturity of what it really means to be a real man. I've made it through the turbulent storms of prison life, and now I look for sunshine and a stars-and-moonlight future filled with sobriety, love, respect for God, the law, my family, and my fellow man. I know now that a man doesn't do what others do or what his friends do, nor does he sell and use drugs or hurt the people he claims to love with deceptions, lies, anger, violence, and hate.

A real man would never choose any of this over his family, lady, or any of his loved ones. A real man accepts his responsibility for his choices in life. Therefore, my service behind prison walls means that I've accepted mine by serving my time in prison to pay for my indiscretions and crimes against society. I tried many times to excuse myself from all the blame for the crimes I committed. Bottom line is, I made a conscious decision to turn to drugs and alcohol to medicate or mask my pain and sick living problem when I should have opened up to my girlfriend and told her of my pain and problems in life.

One of many of my painful and problematic memories in life that made me want to mask my pain with drugs and alcohol was when I would sit up at night after night and watch my girlfriend suffer through many various sicknesses. I thank God, though, she is better now. At the time when she was suffering, I suffered, too, in quiet silence, when I should have opened up to her and told her of my pain and other problems in life. Perhaps then, both of us could have taken the problem to God in prayer. If I had trusted my girlfriend to understand my pain and trusted that God could and would deliver me of my problems, if I asked, then I wouldn't have turned to the drugs and alcohol that led me down a road of chaotic crime, causing me to become saturated and engulfed in the desire for carnal, secular worldly things, which cause man to fall prey to all manners of material secular sin.

Now I thank God for his constant help in my time of need. He is my provider every second, every minute, and every hour of every day. I can do nothing without him. I can now say, without any reservations, that God is my rock, refuge, and salvation. Jesus is my king and my prison time away from home was a good thing. I'm glad not to be in a grave, you see. At least from prison, I have a second chance to live my life rehabilitated and free.

* * * * *

Cambridge City, Indiana
David M.

I found myself at the age of ten looking down at my dad's casket. I felt love and the reason for life were no longer there, for the love I knew in life was my father, and now he was gone. I confessed to give my life to the devil at that moment in actual words. I didn't want to be loved or accepted by anyone or anything in life. Hatred fueled my soul, and it was all I knew. The devil then took it to be his personal duty to destroy my young life. Alcohol and drugs consumed my vision and everyday thoughts. Therefore, I lost purpose, vision, focus, and direction in life.

At the age of thirty-six, I have found that the love of Jesus can overcome any and all obstacles in life, for when I looked back, I understood Jesus's love saw me through my times of hurt and despair; for I know now that Jesus loved me and was always my protector in life. Now God is my only and all high.

Amen.

* * * * *

Morristown, Tennessee
John P.

When I was only sixteen years old, I started using powder cocaine and alcohol. I was married and even had kids when I was just a kid myself. The drugs and alcohol took control of my life. I lost my wife and kids—I mean, my whole, entire family—by the time I was eighteen years old. I was doing between one and two eight-balls a day. I would rob, cheat, and steal. I would do anything to get it. By the time I was twenty-one years old, I had been married four times and on the verge of yet another divorce.

I met my fifth wife, Linda. She had something I wanted, and that was God. Linda never gave up on me. Through the fire and through the rain she remained. Her unfailing love always would be there to keep me sane. Things got so bad after our third child was born that I was ready to give up and quit on everybody. Then I found out that our baby girl had cancer and I had nowhere else to look, except the Almighty God himself. I fell down on my knees and asked for God's forgiveness, and God said yes to me, and I never craved or felt any desire at all for cocaine or alcohol ever again. Therefore, I thank God for my sobriety today.

Amen.

* * * * *

Sweetwater, Tennessee

I was in the wilderness of life for forty-nine years before I finally surrendered to my Lord, forty-nine years of sinning, breaking the law, five failed marriages, and alcohol and drug addiction. Everything was so bad three of my four children won't even have anything to do with me. God surely didn't put me in prison, but he and I have certainly taken advantage of the situation! For some reason, known only to God, I gave myself to him in June 2003 at Brushy Mountain Prison. I asked him to forgive me and to accept me as I did him.

I was overcome with a feeling of peace like I have never known; no drugs had ever given me that feeling, and believe me, I have tried about every drug in Satan's arsenal. God lifted the bonds of hatred and anger from me. As for my addictions and sinful nature, I am still tempted constantly by every kind of demon you can imagine. If someone angers me or seems to be a threat to me, my first reaction is to kill them. The demons say, "You've done it before. Are you going to let them talk to you that way?"

Well, the old me wasn't filed with love, wisdom, or forgiveness. I would have just reacted instantly without really thinking. The fear of God is the beginning of understanding. To obey him, you have to have an understanding of other people. Just because you are saved doesn't mean other folks have changed!

Once you have love and wisdom in your heart, life is so much better. You find yourself loving people you would have hated before. When you live for him, you are not so spiteful, nor do you judge others the way you did before. When you let God into your life, you are a new person. Whatever you do, though, don't think Satan will give you up that easy. Once you start to live for God, and not him, he works "overtime" trying to get you back! He wants to steal your love, your peace, and your happiness. He's not going to rest, so you can't let down your guard.

Not only will he come at you, but he will send every demon and temptation he can think of. If you ever give in to just one, he really starts to beat down on you. So love God, obey God, and worship *him*. Live for him, and *he* will build you into a stronger, happier person. You will have your free will back to make the right decisions. When you leave this earthly body, he will have a permanent home waiting for you for eternity. So remember to thank him and praise him for all that he gives you.

* * * * *

CLIFFORD HUMPHREY

Seymour, Indiana

My name is Doug. I'm thirty-three years old and am serving a ten-year sentence because of my former addiction to crack cocaine. I was brought up in the church as a child but slipped away from God in later years. I started my freshman year in high school with a little weed, which had a small effect but nothing major. After high school I always worked and smoked weed. Then I got into pills, alcohol, and cocaine. That was when the problems started.

I was always in control, or so I thought, until I tried crack; then my life and the people around me fell apart very fast. I was pulled into a world of drugs and people who use people to get drugs. In eight months I lost all my friends and over twenty-thousand dollars and nearly my life to crack cocaine. Now I'm losing my freedom for ten years.

At one point I turned to suicide to end my problem and almost succeeded, but God had other plans, and I was saved from hell. I take my life day to day and look for God's purpose in me. Not to go into a lot of details, but I was clinically dead with nothing but brain activity for four days, and only by the grace of God did I wake up. Now, after I get through this test sometime soon, I'll find God's purpose for me in life. Whatever it is, I know it doesn't include drugs and alcohol.

About the Author

CLIFFORD HUMPHREY WAS BORN AND raised in Chattanooga, Tennessee. He is a true believer of Jesus Christ.

CPSIA information can be obtained
at www.ICGtesting.com
Printed in the USA
LVHW090448181120
672003LV00008B/810